THE MERRY WIVES OF WINDSOR

WILLIAM SHAKESPEARE

Published by True Sign Publishing House
Address: SY. No. 21/2 & 21/3, Sonnenahalli,
Krishnarajapura, Bengaluru,
Karnataka - 560049 India
E-mail: truesignbooks@gmail.com
Website: www.truesign.in

The Merry Wives of Windsor
Author: William Shakespeare

ISBN: 978-93-5462-742-2

First Edition: 2022

Contents

Dramatis Personae

SIR JOHN FALSTAFF	
FENTON	a young gentleman
SHALLOW	a country justice
SLENDER	cousin to Shallow
FORD	a Gentleman dwelling at Windsor
PAGE	a Gentleman dwelling at Windsor
WILLIAM PAGE	a boy, son to Page
SIR HUGH EVANS	a Welsh parson
DOCTOR CAIUS	a French physician
HOST	of the Garter Inn
BARDOLPH, PISTOL,	
NYM	Followers of Falstaff
ROBIN	page to Falstaff
SIMPLE	servant to Slender
RUGBY	servant to Doctor Caius
MISTRESS FORD	
MISTRESS PAGE	
MISTRESS ANNE PAGE	her daughter, in love with Fenton
MISTRESS QUICKLY	servant to Doctor Caius
SERVANTS	to Page, Ford, &c.

SCENE: Windsor and the neighbourhood

ACT-I
SCENE-I — Windsor. Before Page's house

[*Enter* JUSTICE SHALLOW, SLENDER, *and* SIR HUGH EVANS.]

SHALLOW Sir Hugh, persuade me not; I will make a Star Chamber matter of it; if he were twenty Sir John Falstaffs, he shall not abuse Robert Shallow, esquire.

SLENDER In the county of Gloucester, Justice of Peace, and "coram."

SHALLOW Ay, cousin Slender, and "cust-alorum."

SLENDER Ay, and "rato-lorum" too; and a gentleman born, Master Parson, who writes himself "armigero" in any bill, warrant, quittance, or obligation — "armigero."

SHALLOW Ay, that I do; and have done any time these three hundred years.

SLENDER All his successors, gone before him, hath done't; and all his ancestors, that come after him, may: they may give the dozen white luces in their coat.

SHALLOW It is an old coat.

EVANS The dozen white louses do become an old coat well; it agrees well, passant; it is a familiar beast to man, and signifies love.

SHALLOW The luce is the fresh fish; the salt fish is an old coat.

SLENDER I may quarter, coz?

SHALLOW You may, by marrying.

EVANS It is marring indeed, if he quarter it.

SHALLOW Not a whit.

EVANS Yes, py'r lady! If he has a quarter of your coat, there is but three skirts for yourself, in my simple conjectures; but that is all one. If Sir John Falstaff have committed disparagements unto you, I am of the church, and will be glad to do my benevolence to make atonements and compremises between you.

SHALLOW The Council shall hear it; it is a riot.

EVANS It is not meet the Council hear a riot; there is no fear of Got in a riot; the Council, look you, shall desire to hear the fear of Got, and not to hear a riot; take your vizaments in that.

SHALLOW Ha! o' my life, if I were young again, the sword should end it.

EVANS It is petter that friends is the sword and end it; and there is also another device in my prain, which peradventure prings goot discretions with it. There is Anne Page, which is daughter to Master George Page, which is pretty virginity.

SLENDER Mistress Anne Page? She has brown hair, and speaks small like a woman.

EVANS It is that fery person for all the orld, as just as you will desire; and seven hundred pounds of moneys, and gold, and silver, is her grandsire upon his death's-bed — Got deliver to a joyful resurrections! — give, when she is able to overtake seventeen years old. It were a goot motion if we leave our pribbles and prabbles, and desire a marriage between Master Abraham and Mistress Anne Page.

SHALLOW Did her grandsire leave her seven hundred pound?

EVANS Ay, and her father is make her a petter penny

SHALLOW I know the young gentlewoman; she has good gifts.

EVANS Seven hundred pounds, and possibilities, is goot gifts.

SHALLOW Well, let us see honest Master Page. Is Falstaff there?

EVANS Shall I tell you a lie? I do despise a liar as I do despise one that is false; or as I despise one that is not true. The knight Sir John is there; and, I beseech you, be ruled by your well-willers. I will peat the door for Master Page.

[*Knocks.*]

What, hoa! Got pless your house here!

PAGE *[Within]* Who's there?

EVANS Here is Got's plessing, and your friend, and Justice Shallow; and here young Master Slender, that peradventures shall tell you another tale, if matters grow to your likings.

[*Enter* PAGE.]

PAGE I am glad to see your worships well. I thank you for my venison, Master Shallow.

SHALLOW Master Page, I am glad to see you; much good do it your good heart! I wished your venison better; it was ill killed. How doth good Mistress Page? — and I thank you always with my heart, la! with my heart.

PAGE Sir, I thank you.

SHALLOW Sir, I thank you; by yea and no, I do.

PAGE I am glad to see you, good Master Slender.

SLENDER How does your fallow greyhound, sir? I heard say he was outrun on Cotsall.

PAGE It could not be judged, sir.

SLENDER You'll not confess, you'll not confess.

SHALLOW That he will not: 'tis your fault; 'tis your fault. 'Tis a good dog.

PAGE A cur, sir.

SHALLOW Sir, he's a good dog, and a fair dog; can there be more said? he is good, and fair. Is Sir John Falstaff here?

PAGE Sir, he is within; and I would I could do a good office between you.

EVANS It is spoke as a Christians ought to speak.

SHALLOW He hath wronged me, Master Page.

PAGE Sir, he doth in some sort confess it.

SHALLOW If it be confessed, it is not redressed: is not that so, Master Page? He hath wronged me; indeed he hath; — at a word, he hath, — believe me; Robert Shallow, esquire, saith he is wronged.

PAGE Here comes Sir John.

[*Enter* SIR JOHN FALSTAFF, BARDOLPH, NYM, *and* PISTOL.]

FALSTAFF Now, Master Shallow, you'll complain of me to the King?

SHALLOW Knight, you have beaten my men, killed my deer, and broke open my lodge.

FALSTAFF But not kiss'd your keeper's daughter?

SHALLOW Tut, a pin! this shall be answered.

FALSTAFF I will answer it straight: I have done all this. That is now answered.

SHALLOW The Council shall know this.

FALSTAFF 'Twere better for you if it were known in counsel: you'll be laughed at.

EVANS Pauca verba, Sir John; goot worts.

FALSTAFF Good worts! good cabbage! Slender, I broke your head; what matter have you against me?

SLENDER Marry, sir, I have matter in my head against you; and against your cony-catching rascals, Bardolph, Nym, and Pistol. They carried me to the tavern, and made me drunk, and afterwards picked my pocket.

BARDOLPH You Banbury cheese!

SLENDER Ay, it is no matter.

PISTOL How now, Mephostophilus!

SLENDER Ay, it is no matter.

NYM Slice, I say! pauca, pauca; slice! That's my humour.

SLENDER Where's Simple, my man? Can you tell, cousin?

EVANS Peace, I pray you. Now let us understand. There is three umpires in this matter, as I understand: that is — Master Page, fidelicet Master Page; and there is myself, fidelicet myself; and the three party is, lastly and finally, mine host of the Garter.

PAGE We three to hear it and end it between them.

EVANS Fery goot: I will make a prief of it in my note-book; and we will afterwards ork upon the cause with as great discreetly as we can.

FALSTAFF Pistol!

PISTOL He hears with ears.

EVANS	The tevil and his tam! what phrase is this, "He hears with ear"? Why, it is affectations.
FALSTAFF	Pistol, did you pick Master Slender's purse?
SLENDER	Ay, by these gloves, did he — or I would I might never come in mine own great chamber again else! — of seven groats in mill-sixpences, and two Edward shovel-boards that cost me two shilling and two pence a-piece of Yead Miller, by these gloves.
FALSTAFF	Is this true, Pistol?
EVANS	No, it is false, if it is a pick-purse.
PISTOL	Ha, thou mountain-foreigner! — Sir John and master mine, I combat challenge of this latten bilbo. Word of denial in thy labras here! Word of denial! Froth and scum, thou liest.
SLENDER	By these gloves, then, 'twas he.
NYM	Be avised, sir, and pass good humours; I will say "marry trap" with you, if you run the nuthook's humour on me; that is the very note of it.
SLENDER	By this hat, then, he in the red face had it; for though I cannot remember what I did when you made me drunk, yet I am not altogether an ass.
FALSTAFF	What say you, Scarlet and John?
BARDOLPH	Why, sir, for my part, I say the gentleman had drunk himself out of his five sentences.
EVANS	It is his "five senses"; fie, what the ignorance is!
BARDOLPH	And being fap, sir, was, as they say, cashier'd; and so conclusions passed the careires.
SLENDER	Ay, you spake in Latin then too; but 'tis no matter; I'll ne'er be drunk whilst I live again, but in honest, civil, godly company, for this trick; if I be drunk, I'll be drunk with those that have the fear of God, and not with drunken knaves.
EVANS	So Got udge me, that is a virtuous mind.
FALSTAFF	You hear all these matters denied, gentlemen; you hear it.

[*Enter* ANNE PAGE *with wine;* MISTRESS FORD *and* MISTRESS PAGE, *following.*]

PAGE — Nay, daughter, carry the wine in; we'll drink within.

[*Exit* ANNE PAGE.]

SLENDER — O heaven! this is Mistress Anne Page.

PAGE — How now, Mistress Ford!

FALSTAFF — Mistress Ford, by my troth, you are very well met; by your leave, good mistress. *[Kissing her]*

PAGE — Wife, bid these gentlemen welcome. Come, we have a hot venison pasty to dinner; come, gentlemen, I hope we shall drink down all unkindness.

[*Exeunt all but* SHALLOW, SLENDER, *and* EVANS.]

SLENDER — I had rather than forty shillings I had my Book of Songs and Sonnets here.

[*Enter* SIMPLE.]

How, Simple! Where have you been? I must wait on myself, must I? You have not the Book of Riddles about you, have you?

SIMPLE — Book of Riddles! why, did you not lend it to Alice Shortcake upon Allhallowmas last, a fortnight afore Michaelmas?

SHALLOW — Come, coz; come, coz; we stay for you. A word with you, coz; marry, this, coz: there is, as 'twere, a tender, a kind of tender, made afar off by Sir Hugh here: do you understand me?

SLENDER — Ay, sir, you shall find me reasonable; if it be so, I shall do that that is reason.

SHALLOW — Nay, but understand me.

SLENDER — So I do, sir.

EVANS — Give ear to his motions, Master Slender: I will description the matter to you, if you pe capacity of it.

SLENDER — Nay, I will do as my cousin Shallow says; I pray you pardon me; he's a justice of peace in his country, simple though I stand here.

EVANS	But that is not the question; the question is concerning your marriage.
SHALLOW	Ay, there's the point, sir.
EVANS	Marry is it; the very point of it; to Mistress Anne Page.
SLENDER	Why, if it be so, I will marry her upon any reasonable demands.
EVANS	But can you affection the 'oman? Let us command to know that of your mouth or of your lips; for divers philosophers hold that the lips is parcel of the mouth: therefore, precisely, can you carry your good will to the maid?
SHALLOW	Cousin Abraham Slender, can you love her?
SLENDER	I hope, sir, I will do as it shall become one that would do reason.
EVANS	Nay, Got's lords and his ladies! you must speak possitable, if you can carry her your desires towards her.
SHALLOW	That you must. Will you, upon good dowry, marry her?
SLENDER	I will do a greater thing than that upon your request, cousin, in any reason.
SHALLOW	Nay, conceive me, conceive me, sweet coz; what I do is to pleasure you, coz. Can you love the maid?
SLENDER	I will marry her, sir, at your request; but if there be no great love in the beginning, yet heaven may decrease it upon better acquaintance, when we are married and have more occasion to know one another; I hope upon familiarity will grow more contempt. But if you say "Marry her," I will marry her; that I am freely dissolved, and dissolutely.
EVANS	It is a fery discretion answer; save, the fall is in the ort "dissolutely:" the ort is, according to our meaning, "resolutely." His meaning is good.
SHALLOW	Ay, I think my cousin meant well.
SLENDER	Ay, or else I would I might be hanged, la!
SHALLOW	Here comes fair Mistress Anne.

[*Re-enter* ANNE PAGE.]

	Would I were young for your sake, Mistress Anne!

ANNE — The dinner is on the table; my father desires your worships' company.

SHALLOW — I will wait on him, fair Mistress Anne!

EVANS — Od's plessed will! I will not be absence at the grace.

[*Exeunt* SHALLOW *and* EVANS.]

ANNE — Will't please your worship to come in, sir?

SLENDER — No, I thank you, forsooth, heartily; I am very well.

ANNE — The dinner attends you, sir.

SLENDER — I am not a-hungry, I thank you, forsooth. Go, sirrah, for all you are my man, go wait upon my cousin Shallow.

[*Exit* SIMPLE.]

A justice of peace sometime may be beholding to his friend for a man. I keep but three men and a boy yet, till my mother be dead. But what though? Yet I live like a poor gentleman born.

ANNE — I may not go in without your worship: they will not sit till you come.

SLENDER — I' faith, I'll eat nothing; I thank you as much as though I did.

ANNE — I pray you, sir, walk in.

SLENDER — I had rather walk here, I thank you. I bruised my shin th' other day with playing at sword and dagger with a master of fence; three veneys for a dish of stewed prunes — and, by my troth, I cannot abide the smell of hot meat since. Why do your dogs bark so? Be there bears i' the town?

ANNE — I think there are, sir; I heard them talked of.

SLENDER — I love the sport well; but I shall as soon quarrel at it as any man in England. You are afraid, if you see the bear loose, are you not?

ANNE — Ay, indeed, sir.

SLENDER — That's meat and drink to me now. I have seen Sackerson loose twenty times, and have taken him by the chain; but I warrant you, the women have so cried and shrieked at it that it passed; but women, indeed, cannot abide 'em; they are very ill-favoured rough things.

[*Re-enter* PAGE.]

PAGE Come, gentle Master Slender, come; we stay for you.

SLENDER I'll eat nothing, I thank you, sir.

PAGE By cock and pie, you shall not choose, sir! come, come.

SLENDER Nay, pray you lead the way.

PAGE Come on, sir.

SLENDER Mistress Anne, yourself shall go first.

ANNE Not I, sir; pray you keep on.

SLENDER Truly, I will not go first; truly, la! I will not do you that wrong.

ANNE I pray you, sir.

SLENDER I'll rather be unmannerly than troublesome. You do yourself wrong indeed, la!

[*Exeunt.*]

SCENE-II — The same

[*Enter* SIR HUGH EVANS *and* SIMPLE.]

EVANS — Go your ways, and ask of Doctor Caius' house which is the way; and there dwells one Mistress Quickly, which is in the manner of his nurse, or his dry nurse, or his cook, or his laundry, his washer, and his wringer.

SIMPLE — Well, sir.

EVANS — Nay, it is petter yet. Give her this letter; for it is a 'oman that altogether's acquaintance with Mistress Anne Page; and the letter is to desire and require her to solicit your master's desires to Mistress Anne Page. I pray you be gone: I will make an end of my dinner; there's pippins and cheese to come.

[*Exeunt.*]

SCENE-III — A room in the Garter Inn

[*Enter* FALSTAFF, HOST, BARDOLPH, NYM, PISTOL, *and* ROBIN.]

FALSTAFF Mine host of the Garter!

HOST What says my bully rook? Speak scholarly and wisely.

FALSTAFF Truly, mine host, I must turn away some of my followers.

HOST Discard, bully Hercules; cashier; let them wag; trot, trot.

FALSTAFF I sit at ten pounds a week.

HOST Thou'rt an emperor, Caesar, Keiser, and Pheazar. I will entertain Bardolph; he shall draw, he shall tap; said I well, bully Hector?

FALSTAFF Do so, good mine host.

HOST I have spoke; let him follow. [To BARDOLPH] Let me see thee froth and lime. I am at a word; follow.

[*Exit* HOST.]

FALSTAFF Bardolph, follow him. A tapster is a good trade; an old cloak makes a new jerkin; a withered serving-man a fresh tapster. Go; adieu.

BARDOLPH It is a life that I have desired; I will thrive.

PISTOL O base Hungarian wight! Wilt thou the spigot wield?

[*Exit* BARDOLPH.]

NYM He was gotten in drink. Is not the humour conceited?

FALSTAFF I am glad I am so acquit of this tinder-box: his thefts were too open; his filching was like an unskilful singer — he kept not time.

NYM The good humour is to steal at a minim's rest.

PISTOL "Convey" the wise it call. "Steal!" foh! A fico for the phrase!

FALSTAFF Well, sirs, I am almost out at heels.

PISTOL Why, then, let kibes ensue.

FALSTAFF There is no remedy; I must cony-catch; I must shift.

PISTOL Young ravens must have food.

FALSTAFF Which of you know Ford of this town?

PISTOL I ken the wight; he is of substance good.

FALSTAFF My honest lads, I will tell you what I am about.

PISTOL Two yards, and more.

FALSTAFF No quips now, Pistol. Indeed, I am in the waist two yards about; but I am now about no waste; I am about thrift. Briefly, I do mean to make love to Ford's wife; I spy entertainment in her; she discourses, she carves, she gives the leer of invitation; I can construe the action of her familiar style; and the hardest voice of her behaviour, to be Englished rightly, is "I am Sir John Falstaff's."

PISTOL He hath studied her will, and translated her will out of honesty into English.

NYM The anchor is deep; will that humour pass?

FALSTAFF Now, the report goes she has all the rule of her husband's purse; he hath a legion of angels.

PISTOL As many devils entertain; and "To her, boy," say I.

NYM The humour rises; it is good; humour me the angels.

FALSTAFF I have writ me here a letter to her; and here another to Page's wife, who even now gave me good eyes too, examined my parts with most judicious oeillades; sometimes the beam of her view gilded my foot, sometimes my portly belly.

PISTOL Then did the sun on dunghill shine.

NYM I thank thee for that humour.

FALSTAFF O! she did so course o'er my exteriors with such a greedy intention that the appetite of her eye did seem to scorch me up like a burning-glass. Here's another letter to her: she bears the purse too; she is a region in Guiana, all gold and bounty. I will be cheator to them both, and they shall be exchequers to me; they shall be my East

	and West Indies, and I will trade to them both. Go, bear thou this letter to Mistress Page; and thou this to Mistress Ford. We will thrive, lads, we will thrive.
PISTOL	Shall I Sir Pandarus of Troy become, And by my side wear steel? then Lucifer take all!
NYM	I will run no base humour. Here, take the humour-letter; I will keep the haviour of reputation.
FALSTAFF	[To Robin] Hold, sirrah; bear you these letters tightly; Sail like my pinnace to these golden shores. Rogues, hence, avaunt! vanish like hailstones, go; Trudge, plod away o' hoof; seek shelter, pack! Falstaff will learn the humour of this age; French thrift, you rogues; myself, and skirted page.

[*Exeunt* Falstaff *and* Robin.]

PISTOL	Let vultures gripe thy guts! for gourd and fullam holds, And high and low beguile the rich and poor; Tester I'll have in pouch when thou shalt lack, Base Phrygian Turk!
NYM	I have operations in my head which be humours of revenge.
PISTOL	Wilt thou revenge?
NYM	By welkin and her star!
PISTOL	With wit or steel?
NYM	With both the humours, I: I will discuss the humour of this love to Page.
PISTOL	And I to Ford shall eke unfold How Falstaff, varlet vile, His dove will prove, his gold will hold, And his soft couch defile.
NYM	My humour shall not cool: I will incense Page to deal with poison; I will possess him with yellowness, for the revolt of mine is dangerous: that is my true humour.
PISTOL	Thou art the Mars of malcontents; I second thee; troop on.

[*Exeunt*.]

SCENE-IV — A room in Doctor Caius's house

[*Enter* MISTRESS QUICKLY, *and* SIMPLE.]

QUICKLY What, John Rugby!

[*Enter* RUGBY.]

I pray thee go to the casement, and see if you can see my master, Master Doctor Caius, coming: if he do, i' faith, and find anybody in the house, here will be an old abusing of God's patience and the King's English.

RUGBY I'll go watch.

QUICKLY Go; and we'll have a posset for't soon at night, in faith, at the latter end of a sea-coal fire.

[*Exit* RUGBY.]

An honest, willing, kind fellow, as ever servant shall come in house withal; and, I warrant you, no tell-tale nor no breed-bate; his worst fault is that he is given to prayer; he is something peevish that way; but nobody but has his fault; but let that pass. Peter Simple you say your name is?

SIMPLE Ay, for fault of a better.

QUICKLY And Master Slender's your master?

SIMPLE Ay, forsooth.

QUICKLY Does he not wear a great round beard, like a glover's paring-knife?

SIMPLE No, forsooth; he hath but a little whey face, with a little yellow beard — a cane-coloured beard.

QUICKLY A softly-sprighted man, is he not?

SIMPLE — Ay, forsooth; but he is as tall a man of his hands as any is between this and his head; he hath fought with a warrener.

QUICKLY — How say you? — O! I should remember him. Does he not hold up his head, as it were, and strut in his gait?

SIMPLE — Yes, indeed, does he.

QUICKLY — Well, heaven send Anne Page no worse fortune! Tell Master Parson Evans I will do what I can for your master: Anne is a good girl, and I wish —

[*Re-enter* RUGBY.]

RUGBY — Out, alas! here comes my master.

QUICKLY — We shall all be shent. Run in here, good young man; go into this closet.

[*Shuts* SIMPLE *in the closet.*]

He will not stay long. What, John Rugby! John! what, John, I say! Go, John, go inquire for my master; I doubt he be not well that he comes not home.

[*Exit Rugby.*]

[*Sings.*] And down, down, adown-a, &c.

[*Enter* DOCTOR CAIUS.]

CAIUS — Vat is you sing? I do not like des toys. Pray you, go and vetch me in my closet une boitine verde — a box, a green-a box: do intend vat I speak? a green-a box.

QUICKLY — Ay, forsooth, I'll fetch it you.
[Aside] I am glad he went not in himself: if he had found the young man, he would have been horn-mad.

CAIUS — Fe, fe, fe fe! ma foi, il fait fort chaud. Je m'en vais a la cour — la grande affaire.

QUICKLY — Is it this, sir?

CAIUS — Oui; mettez le au mon pocket: depechez, quickly — Vere is dat knave, Rugby?

QUICKLY — What, John Rugby? John!

[*Re-enter* RUGBY.]

RUGBY — Here, sir.

CAIUS You are John Rugby, and you are Jack Rugby: come, take-a your rapier, and come after my heel to de court.

RUGBY 'Tis ready, sir, here in the porch.

CAIUS By my trot, I tarry too long — Od's me! Qu'ay j'oublie? Dere is some simples in my closet dat I vill not for the varld I shall leave behind.

QUICKLY [*Aside*] Ay me, he'll find the young man there, and be mad!

CAIUS O diable, diable! vat is in my closet? — Villainy! larron!

[*Pulling* SIMPLE *out*]

Rugby, my rapier!

QUICKLY Good master, be content.

CAIUS Verefore shall I be content-a?

QUICKLY The young man is an honest man.

CAIUS What shall de honest man do in my closet? dere is no honest man dat shall come in my closet.

QUICKLY I beseech you, be not so phlegmatic. Hear the truth of it: he came of an errand to me from Parson Hugh.

CAIUS Vell.

SIMPLE Ay, forsooth, to desire her to —

QUICKLY Peace, I pray you.

CAIUS Peace-a your tongue! — Speak-a your tale.

SIMPLE To desire this honest gentlewoman, your maid, to speak a good word to Mistress Anne Page for my master, in the way of marriage.

QUICKLY This is all, indeed, la! but I'll ne'er put my finger in the fire, and need not.

CAIUS Sir Hugh send-a you? — Rugby, baillez me some paper: tarry you a little-a while. [*Writes.*]

QUICKLY I am glad he is so quiet: if he had been throughly moved, you should have heard him so loud and so melancholy. But notwithstanding, man, I'll do you your master what good I can; and the very yea and the no is, the French doctor, my master — I may call him my master, look you, for I keep his house; and I wash, wring, brew, bake,

	scour, dress meat and drink, make the beds, and do all myself —
SIMPLE	'Tis a great charge to come under one body's hand.
QUICKLY	Are you avis'd o' that? You shall find it a great charge; and to be up early and down late; but notwithstanding, — to tell you in your ear, — I would have no words of it — my master himself is in love with Mistress Anne Page; but notwithstanding that, I know Anne's mind, that's neither here nor there.
CAIUS	You jack'nape; give-a dis letter to Sir Hugh; by gar, it is a shallenge: I will cut his troat in de Park; and I will teach a scurvy jack-a-nape priest to meddle or make. You may be gone; it is not good you tarry here: by gar, I will cut all his two stones; by gar, he shall not have a stone to throw at his dog.

[*Exit* SIMPLE.]

QUICKLY	Alas, he speaks but for his friend.
CAIUS	It is no matter-a ver dat: — do not you tell-a me dat I shall have Anne Page for myself? By gar, I vill kill de Jack priest; and I have appointed mine host of de Jartiere to measure our weapon. By gar, I vill myself have Anne Page.
QUICKLY	Sir, the maid loves you, and all shall be well. We must give folks leave to prate: what, the good-jer!
CAIUS	Rugby, come to the court vit me. By gar, if I have not Anne Page, I shall turn your head out of my door. Follow my heels, Rugby.

[*Exeunt* CAIUS *and* RUGBY.]

QUICKLY	You shall have An fool's-head of your own. No, I know Anne's mind for that: never a woman in Windsor knows more of Anne's mind than I do; nor can do more than I do with her, I thank heaven.
FENTON	[*Within*] Who's within there? ho!
QUICKLY	Who's there, I trow? Come near the house, I pray you.

[*Enter* FENTON.]

FENTON	How now, good woman! how dost thou?

QUICKLY The better, that it pleases your good worship to ask.

FENTON What news? how does pretty Mistress Anne?

QUICKLY In truth, sir, and she is pretty, and honest, and gentle; and one that is your friend, I can tell you that by the way; I praise heaven for it.

FENTON Shall I do any good, thinkest thou? Shall I not lose my suit?

QUICKLY Troth, sir, all is in His hands above; but notwithstanding, Master Fenton, I'll be sworn on a book she loves you. Have not your worship a wart above your eye?

FENTON Yes, marry, have I; what of that?

QUICKLY Well, thereby hangs a tale; good faith, it is such another Nan; but, I detest, an honest maid as ever broke bread. We had an hour's talk of that wart; I shall never laugh but in that maid's company; — but, indeed, she is given too much to allicholy and musing. But for you — well, go to.

FENTON Well, I shall see her to-day. Hold, there's money for thee; let me have thy voice in my behalf: if thou seest her before me, commend me.

QUICKLY Will I? i' faith, that we will; and I will tell your worship more of the wart the next time we have confidence; and of other wooers.

FENTON Well, farewell; I am in great haste now.

QUICKLY Farewell to your worship. —

[*Exit* FENTON.]

Truly, an honest gentleman; but Anne loves him not; for I know Anne's mind as well as another does. Out upon 't, what have I forgot?

[*Exit*.]

ACT-II
SCENE-I — Before Page's house

[*Enter* MISTRESS PAGE, *with a letter.*]

MRS. PAGE What! have I scaped love-letters in the holiday-time of my beauty, and am I now a subject for them? Let me see.

"Ask me no reason why I love you; for though Love use Reason for his precisian, he admits him not for his counsellor. You are not young, no more am I; go to, then, there's sympathy: you are merry, so am I; ha! ha! then there's more sympathy; you love sack, and so do I; would you desire better sympathy? Let it suffice thee, Mistress Page, at the least, if the love of soldier can suffice, that I love thee. I will not say, pity me: 'tis not a soldier-like phrase; but I say, Love me. By me,

Thine own true knight,
By day or night,
Or any kind of light,
With all his might,
For thee to fight,

JOHN FALSTAFF What a Herod of Jewry is this! O wicked, wicked world! One that is well-nigh worn to pieces with age to show himself a young gallant. What an unweighed behaviour hath this Flemish drunkard picked, with the devil's name! out of my conversation, that he dares in this manner assay me? Why, he hath not been thrice in my company! What should I say to him? I was then frugal of my mirth: — Heaven forgive me!

Why, I'll exhibit a bill in the parliament for the putting down of men. How shall I be revenged on him? for revenged I will be, as sure as his guts are made of puddings.

[*Enter* MISTRESS FORD.]

MRS. FORD — Mistress Page! trust me, I was going to your house.

MRS. PAGE — And, trust me, I was coming to you. You look very ill.

MRS. FORD — Nay, I'll ne'er believe that; I have to show to the contrary.

MRS. PAGE — Faith, but you do, in my mind.

MRS. FORD — Well, I do, then; yet, I say, I could show you to the contrary. O, Mistress Page! give me some counsel.

MRS. PAGE — What's the matter, woman?

MRS. FORD — O woman, if it were not for one trifling respect, I could come to such honour!

MRS. PAGE — Hang the trifle, woman; take the honour. What is it? — Dispense with trifles; — what is it?

MRS. FORD — If I would but go to hell for an eternal moment or so, I could be knighted.

MRS. PAGE — What? thou liest. Sir Alice Ford! These knights will hack; and so thou shouldst not alter the article of thy gentry.

MRS. FORD — We burn daylight: here, read, read; perceive how I might be knighted. I shall think the worse of fat men as long as I have an eye to make difference of men's liking: and yet he would not swear; praised women's modesty; and gave such orderly and well-behaved reproof to all uncomeliness that I would have sworn his disposition would have gone to the truth of his words; but they do no more adhere and keep place together than the Hundredth Psalm to the tune of "Greensleeves." What tempest, I trow, threw this whale, with so many tuns of oil in his belly, ashore at Windsor? How shall I be revenged on him? I think the best way were to entertain him with hope, till the wicked fire of lust have melted him in his own grease. Did you ever hear the like?

MRS. PAGE — Letter for letter, but that the name of Page and Ford differs. To thy great comfort in this mystery of ill opinions, here's the twin-brother of thy letter; but let thine inherit first, for, I protest, mine never shall. I warrant he hath a thousand of these letters, writ with blank space for different names, sure, more, and these are of the second edition. He will print them, out of doubt; for he cares not what he puts into the press, when he would put us two: I had rather be a giantess and lie under Mount Pelion. Well, I will find you twenty lascivious turtles ere one chaste man.

MRS. FORD — Why, this is the very same; the very hand, the very words. What doth he think of us?

MRS. PAGE — Nay, I know not; it makes me almost ready to wrangle with mine own honesty. I'll entertain myself like one that I am not acquainted withal; for, sure, unless he know some strain in me that I know not myself, he would never have boarded me in this fury.

MRS. FORD — "Boarding" call you it? I'll be sure to keep him above deck.

MRS. PAGE — So will I; if he come under my hatches, I'll never to sea again. Let's be revenged on him; let's appoint him a meeting, give him a show of comfort in his suit, and lead him on with a fine-baited delay, till he hath pawned his horses to mine host of the Garter.

MRS. FORD — Nay, I will consent to act any villainy against him that may not sully the chariness of our honesty. O, that my husband saw this letter! It would give eternal food to his jealousy.

MRS. PAGE: Why, look where he comes; and my good man too: he's as far from jealousy as I am from giving him cause; and that, I hope, is an unmeasurable distance.

MRS. FORD: You are the happier woman.

MRS. PAGE: Let's consult together against this greasy knight. Come hither.

[*They retire.*]

[*Enter* FORD, PISTOL, *and* PAGE *and* NYM.]

FORD: Well, I hope it be not so.

PISTOL: Hope is a curtal dog in some affairs:
Sir John affects thy wife.

FORD: Why, sir, my wife is not young.

PISTOL: He woos both high and low, both rich and poor,
Both young and old, one with another, Ford;
He loves the gallimaufry. Ford, perpend.

FORD: Love my wife!

PISTOL: With liver burning hot: prevent, or go thou,
Like Sir Actaeon he, with Ringwood at thy heels.
—
O! odious is the name!

FORD: What name, sir?

PISTOL: The horn, I say. Farewell:
Take heed; have open eye, for thieves do foot by night;
Take heed, ere summer comes, or cuckoo birds do sing.
Away, Sir Corporal Nym.
Believe it, Page; he speaks sense.

[*Exit* PISTOL.]

FORD: [*Aside*] I will be patient: I will find out this.

NYM: [TO PAGE] And this is true; I like not the humour of lying. He hath wronged me in some humours: I should have borne the humoured letter to her; but I have a sword, and it shall bite upon my necessity. He loves your wife; there's the short and the long. My name is Corporal Nym; I speak, and I avouch 'tis true. My name is Nym, and Falstaff loves your wife. Adieu. I love not the humour of bread and cheese; and there's the humour of it. Adieu.

[*Exit* NYM.]

PAGE — [*Aside*] "The humour of it," quoth 'a! Here's a fellow frights English out of his wits.

FORD — I will seek out Falstaff.

PAGE — I never heard such a drawling, affecting rogue.

FORD — If I do find it: well.

PAGE — I will not believe such a Cataian, though the priest o' the town commended him for a true man.

FORD — Twas a good sensible fellow: well.

PAGE — How now, Meg!

[MISTRESS PAGE *and* MISTRESS FORD *come forward.*]

MRS. PAGE — Whither go you, George? — Hark you.

MRS. FORD — How now, sweet Frank! why art thou melancholy?

FORD — I melancholy! I am not melancholy. Get you home, go.

MRS. FORD — Faith, thou hast some crotchets in thy head now. Will you go, Mistress Page?

MRS. PAGE — Have with you. You'll come to dinner, George? [*Aside to* MRS. FORD] Look who comes yonder: she shall be our messenger to this paltry knight.

MRS. FORD — [*Aside to* MRS. PAGE] Trust me, I thought on her: she'll fit it.

[*Enter* MISTRESS QUICKLY.]

MRS. PAGE — You are come to see my daughter Anne?

QUICKLY — Ay, forsooth; and, I pray, how does good Mistress Anne?

MRS. PAGE — Go in with us and see; we'd have an hour's talk with you.

[*Exeunt* MISTRESS PAGE, MISTRESS FORD, *and* MISTRESS QUICKLY.]

PAGE How now, Master Ford!

FORD You heard what this knave told me, did you not?

PAGE Yes; and you heard what the other told me?

FORD Do you think there is truth in them?

PAGE Hang 'em, slaves! I do not think the knight would offer it; but these that accuse him in his intent towards our wives are a yoke of his discarded men; very rogues, now they be out of service.

FORD Were they his men?

PAGE Marry, were they.

FORD I like it never the better for that. Does he lie at the Garter?

PAGE Ay, marry, does he. If he should intend this voyage toward my wife, I would turn her loose to him; and what he gets more of her than sharp words, let it lie on my head.

FORD I do not misdoubt my wife; but I would be loath to turn them together. A man may be too confident. I would have nothing "lie on my head": I cannot be thus satisfied.

PAGE Look where my ranting host of the Garter comes. There is either liquor in his pate or money in his purse when he looks so merrily.

[*Enter* HOST *and* SHALLOW.]

How now, mine host!

HOST How now, bully-rook! Thou'rt a gentleman. Cavaliero-justice, I say!

SHALLOW I follow, mine host, I follow. Good even and twenty, good Master Page! Master Page, will you go with us? We have sport in hand.

HOST Tell him, cavaliero-justice; tell him, bully-rook.

SHALLOW Sir, there is a fray to be fought between Sir Hugh the Welsh priest and Caius the French doctor.

FORD Good mine host o' the Garter, a word with you.

HOST What say'st thou, my bully-rook?

[*They go aside.*]

SHALLOW [To PAGE] Will you go with us to behold it? My merry host hath had the measuring of their weapons; and, I think, hath appointed them contrary places; for, believe me, I hear the parson is no jester. Hark, I will tell you what our sport shall be.

[*They converse apart.*]

HOST Hast thou no suit against my knight, my guest-cavaliero?

FORD None, I protest: but I'll give you a pottle of burnt sack to give me recourse to him, and tell him my name is Brook, only for a jest.

HOST My hand, bully; thou shalt have egress and regress; said I well? and thy name shall be Brook. It is a merry knight. Will you go, mynheers?

SHALLOW Have with you, mine host.

PAGE I have heard the Frenchman hath good skill in his rapier.

SHALLOW Tut, sir! I could have told you more. In these times you stand on distance, your passes, stoccadoes, and I know not what: 'tis the heart, Master Page; 'tis here, 'tis here. I have seen the time with my long sword I would have made you four tall fellows skip like rats.

HOST Here, boys, here, here! Shall we wag?

PAGE Have with you. I had rather hear them scold than fight.

[*Exeunt* HOST, SHALLOW, *and* PAGE.]

FORD Though Page be a secure fool, and stands so firmly on his wife's frailty, yet I cannot put off my opinion so easily. She was in his company at Page's house, and what they made there I know not. Well, I will look further into 't; and I have a disguise to sound Falstaff. If I find her honest, I lose not my labour; if she be otherwise, 'tis labour well bestowed.

[*Exit.*]

SCENE-II — A room in the Garter Inn

[*Enter* FALSTAFF *and* PISTOL.]

FALSTAFF I will not lend thee a penny.

PISTOL Why then, the world's mine oyster,
Which I with sword will open.
I will retort the sum in equipage.

FALSTAFF Not a penny. I have been content, sir, you should lay my countenance to pawn; I have grated upon my good friends for three reprieves for you and your coach-fellow, Nym; or else you had looked through the grate, like a geminy of baboons. I am damned in hell for swearing to gentlemen my friends you were good soldiers and tall fellows; and when Mistress Bridget lost the handle of her fan, I took 't upon mine honour thou hadst it not.

PISTOL Didst not thou share? Hadst thou not fifteen pence?

FALSTAFF Reason, you rogue, reason. Thinkest thou I'll endanger my soul gratis? At a word, hang no more about me, I am no gibbet for you: go: a short knife and a throng! — to your manor of Picht-hatch! go. You'll not bear a letter for me, you rogue! — you stand upon your honour! — Why, thou unconfinable baseness, it is as much as I can do to keep the terms of my honour precise. I, I, I myself sometimes, leaving the fear of God on the left hand, and hiding mine honour in my necessity, am fain to shuffle, to hedge, and to lurch; and yet you, rogue, will ensconce your rags, your cat-a-mountain looks, your red-lattice phrases, and your bold-beating oaths, under the shelter of your honour! You will not do it, you!

PISTOL I do relent; what wouldst thou more of man?

[*Enter* ROBIN.]

ROBIN Sir, here's a woman would speak with you.

FALSTAFF Let her approach.

[*Enter* MISTRESS QUICKLY.]

QUICKLY Give your worship good morrow.

FALSTAFF Good morrow, good wife.

QUICKLY Not so, an't please your worship.

FALSTAFF Good maid, then.

QUICKLY I'll be sworn;
As my mother was, the first hour I was born.

FALSTAFF I do believe the swearer. What with me?

QUICKLY Shall I vouchsafe your worship a word or two?

FALSTAFF Two thousand, fair woman; and I'll vouchsafe thee the hearing.

QUICKLY There is one Mistress Ford, sir, — I pray, come a little nearer this ways: — I myself dwell with Master Doctor Caius.

FALSTAFF Well, on: Mistress Ford, you say, —

QUICKLY Your worship says very true; — I pray your worship come a little nearer this ways.

FALSTAFF I warrant thee nobody hears — mine own people, mine own people.

QUICKLY Are they so? God bless them, and make them His servants!

FALSTAFF Well: Mistress Ford, what of her?

QUICKLY Why, sir, she's a good creature. Lord, Lord! your worship's a wanton! Well, heaven forgive you, and all of us, I pray.

FALSTAFF Mistress Ford; come, Mistress Ford —

QUICKLY Marry, this is the short and the long of it. You have brought her into such a canaries as 'tis wonderful: the best courtier of them all, when the court lay at Windsor, could never have brought her to such a canary; yet there has been knights, and lords, and gentlemen, with their coaches; I warrant you, coach after coach, letter after letter, gift after gift; smelling so sweetly, — all musk, and so rushling, I warrant you, in silk and gold; and in such alligant terms; and in such wine and sugar of the best and the fairest, that would have won any woman's heart; and I warrant you, they could never get an eye-wink of her. I had myself twenty angels given me this morning; but I defy all angels, in any such sort, as they say, but in the way of honesty: and, I warrant you, they could never get her so much as sip on a cup with the proudest of them all; and yet there has been earls, nay, which is more, pensioners; but, I warrant you, all is one with her.

FALSTAFF But what says she to me? be brief, my good she-Mercury.

QUICKLY Marry, she hath received your letter; for the which she thanks you a thousand times; and she gives you to notify that her husband will be absence from his house between ten and eleven.

FALSTAFF Ten and eleven?

QUICKLY Ay, forsooth; and then you may come and see the picture, she says, that you wot of: Master Ford, her husband, will be from home. Alas! the sweet woman leads an ill life with him; he's a very jealousy man; she leads a very frampold life with him, good heart.

FALSTAFF Ten and eleven. Woman, commend me to her; I will not fail her.

QUICKLY Why, you say well. But I have another messenger to your worship: Mistress Page hath her hearty commendations to you too; and let me tell you in your ear, she's as fartuous a civil modest wife, and one, I tell you, that will not miss you morning nor evening prayer, as any is in Windsor, whoe'er be the other; and she bade me tell your worship that her husband is seldom from home, but she hopes there will come a time. I never knew a woman so dote upon a man: surely I think you have charms, la! yes, in truth.

FALSTAFF Not I, I assure thee; setting the attraction of my good parts aside, I have no other charms.

QUICKLY Blessing on your heart for 't!

FALSTAFF But, I pray thee, tell me this: has Ford's wife and Page's wife acquainted each other how they love me?

QUICKLY That were a jest indeed! They have not so little grace, I hope: that were a trick indeed! But Mistress Page would desire you to send her your little page, of all loves: her husband has a marvellous infection to the little page; and, truly, Master Page is an honest man. Never a wife in Windsor leads a better life than she does; do what she will, say what she will, take all, pay all, go to bed when she list, rise when she list, all is as she will; and truly she deserves it; for if there be a kind woman in Windsor, she is one. You must send her your page; no remedy.

FALSTAFF Why, I will.

QUICKLY Nay, but do so then; and, look you, he may come and go between you both; and in any case have a nay-word, that you may know one another's mind, and the boy never need to understand any thing; for 'tis not good that children should know any wickedness: old folks, you know, have discretion, as they say, and know the world.

FALSTAFF Fare thee well; commend me to them both. There's my purse; I am yet thy debtor. Boy, go along with this woman. —

[*Exeunt* MISTRESS QUICKLY *and* ROBIN.]

This news distracts me.

PISTOL This punk is one of Cupid's carriers;
Clap on more sails; pursue; up with your fights;
Give fire; she is my prize, or ocean whelm them all!

[*Exit* PISTOL.]

FALSTAFF Say'st thou so, old Jack? go thy ways; I'll make more of thy old body than I have done. Will they yet look after thee? Wilt thou, after the expense of so much money, be now a gainer? Good body, I thank thee. Let them say 'tis grossly done; so it be fairly done, no matter.

[*Enter* BARDOLPH, *with a cup of sack.*]

BARDOLPH Sir John, there's one Master Brook below would fain speak with you and be acquainted with you: and hath sent your worship a morning's draught of sack.

FALSTAFF Brook is his name?

BARDOLPH Ay, sir.

FALSTAFF Call him in.

[*Exit* BARDOLPH.]

Such Brooks are welcome to me, that o'erflow such liquor. Ah, ha! Mistress Ford and Mistress Page, have I encompassed you? Go to; via!

[*Re-enter* BARDOLPH, *with* FORD *disguised.*]

FORD Bless you, sir!

FALSTAFF And you, sir; would you speak with me?

FORD I make bold to press with so little preparation upon you.

FALSTAFF You're welcome. What's your will? — Give us leave, drawer.

[*Exit* BARDOLPH.]

FORD Sir, I am a gentleman that have spent much: my name is Brook.

FALSTAFF Good Master Brook, I desire more acquaintance of you.

FORD Good Sir John, I sue for yours: not to charge you; for I must let you understand I think myself in better plight for a lender than you are: the which hath something embold'ned me to this unseasoned intrusion; for they say, if money go before, all ways do lie open.

FALSTAFF Money is a good soldier, sir, and will on.

FORD Troth, and I have a bag of money here troubles me; if you will help to bear it, Sir John, take all, or half, for easing me of the carriage.

FALSTAFF Sir, I know not how I may deserve to be your porter.

FORD I will tell you, sir, if you will give me the hearing.

FALSTAFF Speak, good Master Brook; I shall be glad to be your servant.

FORD Sir, I hear you are a scholar, — I will be brief with you, and you have been a man long known to me, though I had never so good means, as desire, to make myself acquainted with you. I shall discover a thing to you, wherein I must very much lay open mine own imperfection; but, good Sir John, as you have one eye upon my follies, as you hear them unfolded, turn another into the register of your own, that I may pass with a reproof the easier, sith you yourself know how easy is it to be such an offender.

FALSTAFF Very well, sir; proceed.

FORD There is a gentlewoman in this town, her husband's name is Ford.

FALSTAFF Well, sir.

FORD I have long loved her, and, I protest to you, bestowed much on her; followed her with a doting observance; engrossed opportunities to meet her; fee'd every slight occasion that could but niggardly give me sight of her; not only bought many presents to give her, but have given largely to many to know what she would have given; briefly, I have pursued her as love hath pursued me; which hath been on the wing of all occasions. But whatsoever I have merited, either in my mind or in my means, meed, I am sure, I have received none, unless experience be a jewel that I have purchased at an infinite rate, and that hath taught me to say this,

Love like a shadow flies when substance love pursues;
Pursuing that that flies, and flying what pursues.

FALSTAFF Have you received no promise of satisfaction at her hands?

FORD Never.

FALSTAFF Have you importuned her to such a purpose?

FORD Never.

FALSTAFF Of what quality was your love, then?

FORD Like a fair house built on another man's ground; so that I have lost my edifice by mistaking the place where I erected it.

FALSTAFF To what purpose have you unfolded this to me?

FORD When I have told you that, I have told you all. Some say that though she appear honest to me, yet in other places she enlargeth her mirth so far that there is shrewd construction made of her. Now, Sir John, here is the heart of my purpose: you are a gentleman of excellent breeding, admirable discourse, of great admittance, authentic in your place and person, generally allowed for your many war-like, court-like, and learnèd preparations.

FALSTAFF O, sir!

FORD Believe it, for you know it. There is money; spend it, spend it; spend more; spend all I have; only give me so much of your time in exchange of it as to lay an amiable siege to the honesty of this Ford's wife: use your art of wooing, win her to consent to you; if any man may, you may as soon as any.

FALSTAFF Would it apply well to the vehemency of your affection, that I should win what you would enjoy? Methinks you prescribe to yourself very preposterously.

FORD O, understand my drift. She dwells so securely on the excellency of her honour that the folly of my soul dares not present itself; she is too bright to be looked against. Now, could I come to her with any detection in my hand, my desires had instance and argument to commend themselves; I could drive her then from the ward of her purity, her reputation, her marriage-vow, and a thousand other her defences, which now are too too strongly embattled against me. What say you to't, Sir John?

FALSTAFF Master Brook, I will first make bold with your money; next, give me your hand; and last, as I am a gentleman, you shall, if you will, enjoy Ford's wife.

FORD O good sir!

FALSTAFF I say you shall.

FORD Want no money, Sir John; you shall want none.

FALSTAFF Want no Mistress Ford, Master Brook; you shall want none. I shall be with her, I may tell you, by her own appointment; even as you came in to me her assistant or go-between parted from me: I say I shall be with her between ten and eleven; for at that time the jealous rascally knave, her husband, will be forth. Come you to me at night; you shall know how I speed.

FORD I am blest in your acquaintance. Do you know Ford, sir?

FALSTAFF Hang him, poor cuckoldly knave! I know him not; yet I wrong him to call him poor; they say the jealous wittolly knave hath masses of money; for the which his wife seems to me well-favoured. I will use her as the key of the cuckoldly rogue's coffer; and there's my harvest-home.

FORD I would you knew Ford, sir, that you might avoid him if you saw him.

FALSTAFF Hang him, mechanical salt-butter rogue! I will stare him out of his wits; I will awe him with my cudgel; it shall hang like a meteor o'er the cuckold's horns. Master Brook, thou shalt know I will predominate over the peasant, and thou shalt lie with his wife. Come to me soon at night. Ford's a knave, and I will aggravate his style; thou, Master Brook, shalt know him for knave and cuckold. Come to me soon at night.

[*Exit* FALSTAFF.]

FORD What a damned Epicurean rascal is this! My heart is ready to crack with impatience. Who says this is improvident jealousy? My wife hath sent to him; the hour is fixed; the match is made. Would any man have thought this? See the hell of having a false woman! My bed shall be abused, my coffers ransacked, my reputation gnawn at; and I shall not only receive this villanous wrong, but stand under the adoption of abominable terms, and by him that does me this wrong. Terms! names! Amaimon sounds well; Lucifer, well; Barbason, well; yet they are devils' additions, the names of fiends. But Cuckold! Wittol! — Cuckold! the devil himself hath not such a name. Page is an ass, a secure ass; he will trust his wife; he will not be jealous; I will rather trust a Fleming with my butter, Parson Hugh the Welshman with my cheese, an Irishman with my aqua-vitae bottle, or a thief to walk my ambling gelding, than my wife with herself; then she plots, then she ruminates, then she devises; and what they think in their hearts they may effect, they will break their hearts but they will effect. God be praised for my jealousy! Eleven o'clock the hour. I will prevent this, detect my wife, be revenged on Falstaff, and laugh at Page. I will about it; better three hours too soon than a minute too late. Fie, fie, fie! cuckold! cuckold! cuckold!

[*Exit.*]

SCENE-III — A field near Windsor

[*Enter* CAIUS *and* RUGBY.]

CAIUS Jack Rugby!

RUGBY Sir?

CAIUS Vat is de clock, Jack?

RUGBY 'Tis past the hour, sir, that Sir Hugh promised to meet.

CAIUS By gar, he has save his soul, dat he is no come; he has pray his Pible vell dat he is no come: by gar, Jack Rugby, he is dead already, if he be come.

RUGBY He is wise, sir; he knew your worship would kill him if he came.

CAIUS By gar, de herring is no dead so as I vill kill him. Take your rapier, Jack; I vill tell you how I vill kill him.

RUGBY Alas, sir, I cannot fence!

CAIUS Villany, take your rapier.

RUGBY Forbear; here's company.

[*Enter* HOST, SHALLOW, SLENDER, *and* PAGE.]

HOST Bless thee, bully doctor!

SHALLOW Save you, Master Doctor Caius!

PAGE Now, good Master Doctor!

SLENDER Give you good morrow, sir.

CAIUS Vat be all you, one, two, tree, four, come for?

HOST To see thee fight, to see thee foin, to see thee traverse; to see thee here, to see thee there; to see thee pass thy punto, thy stock, thy reverse, thy distance, thy montant. Is he dead, my Ethiopian? Is he dead, my Francisco? Ha, bully! What says my Aesculapius? my Galen? my heart of elder? Ha! is he dead, bully stale? Is he dead?

CAIUS By gar, he is de coward Jack priest of de world; he is not show his face.

HOST Thou art a Castalion King Urinal! Hector of Greece, my boy!

CAIUS I pray you, bear witness that me have stay six or seven, two, tree hours for him, and he is no come.

SHALLOW He is the wiser man, Master doctor: he is a curer of souls, and you a curer of bodies; if you should fight, you go against the hair of your professions. Is it not true, Master Page?

PAGE Master Shallow, you have yourself been a great fighter, though now a man of peace.

SHALLOW Bodykins, Master Page, though I now be old, and of the peace, if I see a sword out, my finger itches to make one. Though we are justices, and doctors, and churchmen, Master Page, we have some salt of our youth in us; we are the sons of women, Master Page.

PAGE 'Tis true, Master Shallow.

SHALLOW It will be found so, Master Page. Master Doctor Caius, I come to fetch you home. I am sworn of the peace; you have showed yourself a wise physician, and Sir Hugh hath shown himself a wise and patient churchman. You must go with me, Master Doctor.

HOST Pardon, guest-justice. — A word, Monsieur Mockwater.

CAIUS Mock-vater! Vat is dat?

HOST Mockwater, in our English tongue, is valour, bully.

CAIUS By gar, then I have as much mockvater as de Englishman. — Scurvy jack-dog priest! By gar, me vill cut his ears.

HOST He will clapper-claw thee tightly, bully.

CAIUS Clapper-de-claw! Vat is dat?

HOST That is, he will make thee amends.

CAIUS By gar, me do look he shall clapper-de-claw me; for, by gar, me vill have it.

HOST And I will provoke him to't, or let him wag.

CAIUS Me tank you for dat.

HOST	And, moreover, bully — but first: Master guest, and Master Page, and eke Cavaliero Slender, go you through the town to Frogmore.

[*Aside to them*]

PAGE	Sir Hugh is there, is he?
HOST	He is there: see what humour he is in; and I will bring the doctor about by the fields. Will it do well?
SHALLOW	We will do it.
PAGE, SHALLOW, and SLENDER	Adieu, good Master Doctor.

[*Exeunt* PAGE, SHALLOW, *and* SLENDER.]

CAIUS	By gar, me vill kill de priest; for he speak for a jack-an-ape to Anne Page.
HOST	Let him die. Sheathe thy impatience; throw cold water on thy choler; go about the fields with me through Frogmore; I will bring thee where Mistress Anne Page is, at a farm-house a-feasting; and thou shalt woo her. Cried I aim! Said I well?
CAIUS	By gar, me tank you for dat: by gar, I love you; and I shall procure-a you de good guest, de earl, de knight, de lords, de gentlemen, my patients.
HOST	For the which I will be thy adversary toward Anne Page: said I well?
CAIUS	By gar, 'tis good; vell said.
HOST	Let us wag, then.
CAIUS	Come at my heels, Jack Rugby.

[*Exeunt.*]

ACT-III
SCENE-I — A field near Frogmore

[*Enter* SIR HUGH EVANS *and* SIMPLE.]

EVANS — I pray you now, good Master Slender's serving-man, and friend Simple by your name, which way have you looked for Master Caius, that calls himself doctor of physic?

SIMPLE — Marry, sir, the pittie-ward, the park-ward, every way; old Windsor way, and every way but the town way.

EVANS — I most fehemently desire you you will also look that way.

SIMPLE — I will, Sir.

[*Exit* SIMPLE.]

EVANS — Pless my soul, how full of chollors I am, and trempling of mind! I shall be glad if he have deceived me. How melancholies I am! I will knog his urinals about his knave's costard when I have goot opportunities for the 'ork: pless my soul!

[*Sings*]

To shallow rivers, to whose falls
Melodious birds sings madrigals;
There will we make our peds of roses,
And a thousand fragrant posies.
To shallow —

Mercy on me! I have a great dispositions to cry.

[*Sings*]

Melodious birds sing madrigals, —
Whenas I sat in Pabylon, —
And a thousand vagram posies.
To shallow, —

[*Re-enter* SIMPLE.]

SIMPLE Yonder he is, coming this way, Sir Hugh.

EVANS He's welcome.

[*Sings*]

To shallow rivers, to whose falls —

Heaven prosper the right! — What weapons is he?

SIMPLE No weapons, sir. There comes my master, Master Shallow, and another gentleman, from Frogmore, over the stile, this way.

EVANS Pray you give me my gown; or else keep it in your arms. [*Reads in a book.*]

[*Enter* PAGE, SHALLOW, *and* SLENDER.]

SHALLOW How now, Master Parson! Good morrow, good Sir Hugh. Keep a gamester from the dice, and a good student from his book, and it is wonderful.

SLENDER [*Aside*] Ah, sweet Anne Page!

PAGE 'Save you, good Sir Hugh!

EVANS Pless you from his mercy sake, all of you!

SHALLOW What, the sword and the word! Do you study them both, Master Parson?

PAGE And youthful still, in your doublet and hose, this raw rheumatic day!

EVANS There is reasons and causes for it.

PAGE We are come to you to do a good office, Master Parson

EVANS Fery well; what is it?

PAGE Yonder is a most reverend gentleman, who, belike having received wrong by some person, is at most odds with his own gravity and patience that ever you saw

SHALLOW I have lived fourscore years and upward; I never heard a man of his place, gravity, and learning, so wide of his own respect.

EVANS What is he?

PAGE I think you know him: Master Doctor Caius, the renowned French physician.

EVANS Got's will and His passion of my heart! I had as lief you would tell me of a mess of porridge.

PAGE Why?

EVANS He has no more knowledge in Hibbocrates and Galen, — and he is a knave besides; a cowardly knave as you would desires to be acquainted withal.

PAGE I warrant you, he's the man should fight with him

SLENDER [*Aside*] O, sweet Anne Page!

SHALLOW It appears so, by his weapons. Keep them asunder; here comes Doctor Caius.

[*Enter* HOST, CAIUS, *and* RUGBY.]

PAGE Nay, good Master Parson, keep in your weapon

SHALLOW So do you, good Master Doctor.

HOST Disarm them, and let them question; let them keep their limbs whole and hack our English.

CAIUS I pray you, let-a me speak a word with your ear: verefore will you not meet-a me?

EVANS [*Aside to* CAIUS] Pray you use your patience; in good time.

CAIUS By gar, you are de coward, de Jack dog, John ape

EVANS [*Aside to* CAIUS] Pray you, let us not be laughing-stogs to other men's humours; I desire you in friendship, and I will one way or other make you amends.
[*Aloud*] I will knog your urinals about your knave's cogscomb for missing your meetings and appointments.

CAIUS Diable! — Jack Rugby, — mine Host de Jarretiere, — have I not stay for him to kill him? Have I not, at de place I did appoint?

EVANS As I am a Christians soul, now, look you, this is the place appointed. I'll be judgment by mine host of the Garter.

HOST Peace, I say, Gallia and Gaullia; French and Welsh, soul-curer and body-curer!

CAIUS Ay, dat is very good; excellent!

HOST Peace, I say! Hear mine host of the Garter. Am I politic? am I subtle? am I a Machiavel? Shall I lose my doctor? No; he gives me the potions and the motions. Shall I lose my parson, my priest, my Sir Hugh? No; he gives me the proverbs and the no-verbs. Give me thy hand, terrestrial; so; — give me thy hand, celestial; so. Boys of art, I have deceived you both; I have directed you to wrong places; your hearts are mighty, your skins are whole, and let burnt sack be the issue. Come, lay their swords to pawn. Follow me, lads of peace; follow, follow, follow.

SHALLOW Trust me, a mad host! — Follow, gentlemen, follow

SLENDER [*Aside*] O, sweet Anne Page!

[*Exeunt* SHALLOW, SLENDER, PAGE, *and* HOST.]

CAIUS Ha, do I perceive dat? Have you make-a de sot of us, ha, ha?

EVANS This is well; he has made us his vlouting-stog. I desire you that we may be friends; and let us knog our prains together to be revenge on this same scall, scurvy, cogging companion, the host of the Garter.

CAIUS By gar, with all my heart. He promise to bring me where is Anne Page; by gar, he deceive me too.

EVANS Well, I will smite his noddles. Pray you follow.

[*Exeunt.*]

SCENE-II — A street in Windsor

[*Enter* MISTRESS PAGE *and* ROBIN.]

MRS. PAGE Nay, keep your way, little gallant: you were wont to be a follower, but now you are a leader. Whether had you rather lead mine eyes, or eye your master's heels?

ROBIN I had rather, forsooth, go before you like a man than follow him like a dwarf.

MRS. PAGE O! you are a flattering boy: now I see you'll be a courtier.

[*Enter* FORD.]

FORD Well met, Mistress Page. Whither go you?

MRS. PAGE Truly, sir, to see your wife. Is she at home?

FORD Ay; and as idle as she may hang together, for want of company. I think, if your husbands were dead, you two would marry.

MRS. PAGE Be sure of that — two other husbands.

FORD Where had you this pretty weathercock?

MRS. PAGE I cannot tell what the dickens his name is my husband had him of. What do you call your knight's name, sirrah?

ROBIN Sir John Falstaff.

FORD Sir John Falstaff!

MRS. PAGE He, he; I can never hit on's name. There is such a league between my good man and he! Is your wife at home indeed?

FORD Indeed she is.

MRS. PAGE By your leave, sir: I am sick till I see her.

[*Exeunt* MRS. PAGE *and* ROBIN.]

FORD — Has Page any brains? Hath he any eyes? Hath he any thinking? Sure, they sleep; he hath no use of them. Why, this boy will carry a letter twenty mile as easy as a cannon will shoot point-blank twelve score. He pieces out his wife's inclination; he gives her folly motion and advantage; and now she's going to my wife, and Falstaff's boy with her. A man may hear this shower sing in the wind: and Falstaff's boy with her! Good plots! They are laid; and our revolted wives share damnation together. Well; I will take him, then torture my wife, pluck the borrowed veil of modesty from the so seeming Mistress Page, divulge Page himself for a secure and wilful Actaeon; and to these violent proceedings all my neighbours shall cry aim. [*Clock strikes.*] The clock gives me my cue, and my assurance bids me search; there I shall find Falstaff. I shall be rather praised for this than mocked; for it is as positive as the earth is firm that Falstaff is there. I will go.

[*Enter* PAGE, SHALLOW, SLENDER, HOST, SIR HUGH EVANS, CAIUS, *and* RUGBY.]

SHALLOW, PAGE, &c — Well met, Master Ford.

FORD — Trust me, a good knot; I have good cheer at home, and I pray you all go with me.

SHALLOW — I must excuse myself, Master Ford.

SLENDER — And so must I, sir; we have appointed to dine with Mistress Anne, and I would not break with her for more money than I'll speak of.

SHALLOW — We have lingered about a match between Anne Page and my cousin Slender, and this day we shall have our answer.

SLENDER — I hope I have your good will, father Page.

PAGE — You have, Master Slender; I stand wholly for you. But my wife, Master doctor, is for you altogether.

CAIUS — Ay, be-gar; and de maid is love-a me: my nursh-a Quickly tell me so mush.

HOST — What say you to young Master Fenton? He capers, he dances, he has eyes of youth, he writes verses, he speaks holiday, he smells April and May; he will carry 't, he will carry 't; 'tis in his buttons; he will carry 't.

PAGE — Not by my consent, I promise you. The gentleman is of no having: he kept company with the wild Prince and Pointz; he is of too high a region, he knows too much. No, he shall not knit a knot in his fortunes with the finger of my substance; if he take her, let him take her simply; the wealth I have waits on my consent, and my consent goes not that way.

FORD — I beseech you, heartily, some of you go home with me to dinner: besides your cheer, you shall have sport; I will show you a monster. Master Doctor, you shall go; so shall you, Master Page; and you, Sir Hugh.

SHALLOW — Well, fare you well; we shall have the freer wooing at Master Page's.

[*Exeunt* SHALLOW *and* SLENDER.]

CAIUS — Go home, John Rugby; I come anon.

[*Exit* RUGBY.]

HOST — Farewell, my hearts; I will to my honest knight Falstaff, and drink canary with him.

[*Exit* HOST.]

FORD — [*Aside*] I think I shall drink in pipe-wine first with him. I'll make him dance.
Will you go, gentles?

ALL — Have with you to see this monster.

[*Exeunt.*]

SCENE III. A room in Ford's house

[*Enter* MISTRESS FORD *and* MISTRESS PAGE.]

MRS. FORD What, John! what, Robert!

MRS. PAGE Quickly, quickly: — Is the buck-basket —

MRS. FORD I warrant. What, Robin, I say!

[*Enter* SERVANTS *with a basket.*]

MRS. PAGE Come, come, come.

MRS. FORD Here, set it down.

MRS. PAGE Give your men the charge; we must be brief.

MRS. FORD Marry, as I told you before, John and Robert, be ready here hard by in the brew-house; and when I suddenly call you, come forth, and, without any pause or staggering, take this basket on your shoulders: that done, trudge with it in all haste, and carry it among the whitsters in Datchet-Mead, and there empty it in the muddy ditch close by the Thames side.

MRS. PAGE You will do it?

MRS. FORD I have told them over and over; they lack no direction. Be gone, and come when you are called.

[*Exeunt* SERVANTS.]

MRS. PAGE Here comes little Robin.

[*Enter* ROBIN.]

MRS. FORD How now, my eyas-musket! what news with you?

ROBIN My Master Sir John is come in at your back-door, Mistress Ford, and requests your company.

MRS. PAGE You little Jack-a-Lent, have you been true to us?

ROBIN Ay, I'll be sworn. My master knows not of your being here, and hath threatened to put me into everlasting liberty, if I tell you of it; for he swears he'll turn me away.

MRS. PAGE Thou 'rt a good boy; this secrecy of thine shall be a tailor to thee, and shall make thee a new doublet and hose. I'll go hide me.

MRS. FORD Do so. Go tell thy master I am alone.

[*Exit* ROBIN.]

Mistress Page, remember you your cue.

MRS. PAGE I warrant thee; if I do not act it, hiss me.

[*Exit* MISTRESS PAGE.]

MRS. FORD Go to, then; we'll use this unwholesome humidity, this gross watery pumpion; we'll teach him to know turtles from jays.

[*Enter* FALSTAFF.]

FALSTAFF "Have I caught thee, my heavenly jewel?" Why, now let me die, for I have lived long enough: this is the period of my ambition: O this blessed hour!

MRS. FORD O, sweet Sir John!

FALSTAFF Mistress Ford, I cannot cog, I cannot prate, Mistress Ford. Now shall I sin in my wish; I would thy husband were dead. I'll speak it before the best lord, I would make thee my lady.

MRS. FORD I your lady, Sir John! Alas, I should be a pitiful lady

FALSTAFF Let the court of France show me such another. I see how thine eye would emulate the diamond; thou hast the right arched beauty of the brow that becomes the ship-tire, the tire-valiant, or any tire of Venetian admittance.

MRS. FORD A plain kerchief, Sir John; my brows become nothing else; nor that well neither.

FALSTAFF By the Lord, thou art a traitor to say so: thou wouldst make an absolute courtier; and the firm fixture of thy foot would give an excellent motion to thy gait in a semi-circled farthingale. I see what thou wert, if

	Fortune thy foe were not, Nature thy friend. Come, thou canst not hide it.
MRS. FORD	Believe me, there's no such thing in me.
FALSTAFF	What made me love thee? Let that persuade thee there's something extraordinary in thee. Come, I cannot cog and say thou art this and that, like a many of these lisping hawthorn-buds that come like women in men's apparel, and smell like Bucklersbury in simple-time; I cannot; but I love thee, none but thee; and thou deservest it.
MRS. FORD	Do not betray me, sir; I fear you love Mistress Page
FALSTAFF	Thou mightst as well say I love to walk by the Counter-gate, which is as hateful to me as the reek of a lime-kiln.
MRS. FORD	Well, heaven knows how I love you; and you shall one day find it.
FALSTAFF	Keep in that mind; I'll deserve it.
MRS. FORD	Nay, I must tell you, so you do; or else I could not be in that mind.
ROBIN	[*Within*] Mistress Ford! Mistress Ford! here's Mistress Page at the door, sweating and blowing and looking wildly, and would needs speak with you presently.
FALSTAFF	She shall not see me; I will ensconce me behind the arras.
MRS. FORD	Pray you, do so; she's a very tattling woman.

[FALSTAFF *hides himself.*]

[*Re-enter* MISTRESS PAGE *and* ROBIN.]

What's the matter? How now!

MRS. PAGE	O Mistress Ford, what have you done? You're shamed, you are overthrown, you are undone for ever!
MRS. FORD	What's the matter, good Mistress Page?
MRS. PAGE	O well-a-day, Mistress Ford! having an honest man to your husband, to give him such cause of suspicion!
MRS. FORD	What cause of suspicion?
MRS. PAGE	What cause of suspicion? Out upon you! how am I mistook in you!
MRS. FORD	Why, alas, what's the matter?

MRS. PAGE Your husband's coming hither, woman, with all the officers in Windsor, to search for a gentleman that he says is here now in the house, by your consent, to take an ill advantage of his absence: you are undone.

MRS. FORD [*Aside*] Speak louder.
'Tis not so, I hope.

MRS. PAGE Pray heaven it be not so that you have such a man here! but 'tis most certain your husband's coming, with half Windsor at his heels, to search for such a one. I come before to tell you. If you know yourself clear, why, I am glad of it; but if you have a friend here, convey, convey him out. Be not amazed; call all your senses to you; defend your reputation, or bid farewell to your good life for ever.

MRS. FORD What shall I do? — There is a gentleman, my dear friend; and I fear not mine own shame as much as his peril: I had rather than a thousand pound he were out of the house.

MRS. PAGE For shame! never stand "you had rather" and "you had rather": your husband's here at hand; bethink you of some conveyance; in the house you cannot hide him. O, how have you deceived me! Look, here is a basket; if he be of any reasonable stature, he may creep in here; and throw foul linen upon him, as if it were going to bucking: or — it is whiting-time — send him by your two men to Datchet-Mead.

MRS. FORD He's too big to go in there. What shall I do?

FALSTAFF [*Coming forward*] Let me see 't, let me see 't. O, let me see 't! I'll in, I'll in; follow your friend's counsel; I'll in.

MRS. PAGE What, Sir John Falstaff! Are these your letters, knight?

FALSTAFF I love thee and none but thee; help me away: let me creep in here. I'll never —

[*He gets into the basket; they cover him with foul linen.*]

MRS. PAGE Help to cover your master, boy. Call your men, Mistress Ford. You dissembling knight!

MRS. FORD What, John! Robert! John!

[*Exit* ROBIN.]

[*Re-enter* SERVANTS.]

Go, take up these clothes here, quickly; where's the cowl-staff? Look how you drumble! Carry them to the laundress in Datchet-Mead; quickly, come.

[*Enter* FORD, PAGE, CAIUS, *and* SIR HUGH EVANS.]

FORD — Pray you come near. If I suspect without cause, why then make sport at me, then let me be your jest; I deserve it. How now, whither bear you this?

SERVANT — To the laundress, forsooth.

MRS. FORD — Why, what have you to do whither they bear it? You were best meddle with buck-washing.

FORD — Buck! I would I could wash myself of the buck! Buck, buck, buck! ay, buck; I warrant you, buck; and of the season too, it shall appear.

[*Exeunt* SERVANTS *with the basket.*]

Gentlemen, I have dreamed to-night; I'll tell you my dream. Here, here, here be my keys: ascend my chambers; search, seek, find out. I'll warrant we'll unkennel the fox. Let me stop this way first. [*Locking the door*] So, now uncape.

PAGE — Good Master Ford, be contented: you wrong yourself too much.

FORD — True, Master Page. Up, gentlemen, you shall see sport anon; follow me, gentlemen.

[*Exit* FORD.]

EVANS — This is fery fantastical humours and jealousies.

CAIUS — By gar, 'tis no the fashion of France; it is not jealous in France.

PAGE — Nay, follow him, gentlemen; see the issue of his search.

[*Exeunt* EVANS, PAGE, *and* CAIUS.]

MRS. PAGE — Is there not a double excellency in this?

MRS. FORD — I know not which pleases me better, that my husband is deceived, or Sir John.

MRS. PAGE — What a taking was he in when your husband asked who was in the basket!

MRS. FORD — I am half afraid he will have need of washing; so throwing him into the water will do him a benefit.

MRS. PAGE — Hang him, dishonest rascal! I would all of the same strain were in the same distress.

MRS. FORD — I think my husband hath some special suspicion of Falstaff's being here, for I never saw him so gross in his jealousy till now.

MRS. PAGE — I will lay a plot to try that, and we will yet have more tricks with Falstaff: his dissolute disease will scarce obey this medicine.

MRS. FORD — Shall we send that foolish carrion, Mistress Quickly, to him, and excuse his throwing into the water, and give him another hope, to betray him to another punishment?

MRS. PAGE — We will do it; let him be sent for to-morrow eight o'clock, to have amends.

[*Re-enter* FORD, PAGE, CAIUS, *and* SIR HUGH EVANS.]

FORD — I cannot find him: may be the knave bragged of that he could not compass.

MRS. PAGE — [*Aside to* MRS. FORD] Heard you that?

MRS. FORD — [*Aside to* MRS. PAGE] Ay, ay, peace. — You use me well, Master Ford, do you?

FORD — Ay, I do so.

MRS. FORD — Heaven make you better than your thoughts!

FORD — Amen!

MRS. PAGE — You do yourself mighty wrong, Master Ford.

FORD — Ay, ay; I must bear it.

EVANS — If there be any pody in the house, and in the chambers, and in the coffers, and in the presses, heaven forgive my sins at the day of judgment!

CAIUS — Be gar, nor I too; there is no bodies.

PAGE — Fie, fie, Master Ford, are you not ashamed? What spirit, what devil suggests this imagination? I would not ha' your distemper in this kind for the wealth of Windsor Castle.

FORD — 'Tis my fault, Master Page: I suffer for it.

EVANS — You suffer for a pad conscience. Your wife is as honest a 'omans as I will desires among five thousand, and five hundred too.

CAIUS — By gar, I see 'tis an honest woman.

FORD — Well, I promised you a dinner. Come, come, walk in the Park: I pray you pardon me; I will hereafter make known to you why I have done this. Come, wife, come, Mistress Page; I pray you pardon me; pray heartily, pardon me.

PAGE — Let's go in, gentlemen; but, trust me, we'll mock him. I do invite you to-morrow morning to my house to breakfast; after, we'll a-birding together; I have a fine hawk for the bush. Shall it be so?

FORD — Any thing.

EVANS — If there is one, I shall make two in the company.

CAIUS — If there be one or two, I shall make-a the turd.

FORD — Pray you go, Master Page.

EVANS — I pray you now, remembrance to-morrow on the lousy knave, mine host.

CAIUS — Dat is good; by gar, with all my heart.

EVANS — A lousy knave! to have his gibes and his mockeries!

[*Exeunt.*]

SCENE-IV — A room in Page's house

[*Enter* FENTON, ANNE PAGE, *and* MISTRESS QUICKLY. MISTRESS QUICKLY *stands apart.*]

FENTON I see I cannot get thy father's love;
Therefore no more turn me to him, sweet Nan.

ANNE Alas! how then?

FENTON Why, thou must be thyself.
He doth object, I am too great of birth;
And that my state being gall'd with my expense,
I seek to heal it only by his wealth.
Besides these, other bars he lays before me,
My riots past, my wild societies;
And tells me 'tis a thing impossible
I should love thee but as a property.

ANNE May be he tells you true.

FENTON No, heaven so speed me in my time to come!
Albeit I will confess thy father's wealth
Was the first motive that I wooed thee, Anne:
Yet, wooing thee, I found thee of more value
Than stamps in gold, or sums in sealèd bags;
And 'tis the very riches of thyself
That now I aim at.

ANNE Gentle Master Fenton,
Yet seek my father's love; still seek it, sir.
If opportunity and humblest suit
Cannot attain it, why then, — hark you hither.

[*They converse apart.*]

[*Enter* SHALLOW, SLENDER, *and* MISTRESS QUICKLY.]

SHALLOW Break their talk, Mistress Quickly: my kinsman shall speak for himself.

SLENDER I'll make a shaft or a bolt on 't. 'Slid, 'tis but venturing.

SHALLOW Be not dismayed.

SLENDER No, she shall not dismay me. I care not for that, but that I am afeard.

QUICKLY Hark ye; Master Slender would speak a word with you

ANNE I come to him.
[*Aside*] This is my father's choice.
O, what a world of vile ill-favour'd faults
Looks handsome in three hundred pounds a year!

QUICKLY And how does good Master Fenton? Pray you, a word with you.

SHALLOW She's coming; to her, coz. O boy, thou hadst a father!

SLENDER I had a father, Mistress Anne; my uncle can tell you good jests of him. Pray you, uncle, tell Mistress Anne the jest how my father stole two geese out of a pen, good uncle.

SHALLOW Mistress Anne, my cousin loves you.

SLENDER Ay, that I do; as well as I love any woman in Gloucestershire.

SHALLOW He will maintain you like a gentlewoman.

SLENDER Ay, that I will come cut and long-tail, under the degree of a squire.

SHALLOW He will make you a hundred and fifty pounds jointure.

ANNE Good Master Shallow, let him woo for himself.

SHALLOW Marry, I thank you for it; I thank you for that good comfort. She calls you, coz; I'll leave you.

ANNE Now, Master Slender.

SLENDER Now, good Mistress Anne. —

ANNE What is your will?

SLENDER My will! 'od's heartlings, that's a pretty jest indeed! I ne'er made my will yet, I thank heaven; I am not such a sickly creature, I give heaven praise.

ANNE I mean, Master Slender, what would you with me?

SLENDER Truly, for mine own part I would little or nothing with you. Your father and my uncle hath made motions; if it be my luck, so; if not, happy man be his dole! They can tell you how things go better than I can. You may ask your father; here he comes.

[*Enter* PAGE *and* MISTRESS PAGE.]

PAGE — Now, Master Slender: love him, daughter Anne.
Why, how now! what does Master Fenton here?
You wrong me, sir, thus still to haunt my house:
I told you, sir, my daughter is dispos'd of.

FENTON — Nay, Master Page, be not impatient.

MRS. PAGE — Good Master Fenton, come not to my child.

PAGE — She is no match for you.

FENTON — Sir, will you hear me?

PAGE — No, good Master Fenton.
Come, Master Shallow; come, son Slender, in.
Knowing my mind, you wrong me, Master Fenton.

[*Exeunt* PAGE, SHALLOW, *and* SLENDER.]

QUICKLY — Speak to Mistress Page.

FENTON — Good Mistress Page, for that I love your daughter
In such a righteous fashion as I do,
Perforce, against all checks, rebukes, and manners,
I must advance the colours of my love
And not retire: let me have your good will.

ANNE — Good mother, do not marry me to yond fool.

MRS. PAGE — I mean it not; I seek you a better husband.

QUICKLY — That's my master, Master doctor.

ANNE — Alas! I had rather be set quick i' the earth.
And bowl'd to death with turnips.

MRS. PAGE — Come, trouble not yourself. Good Master Fenton,
I will not be your friend, nor enemy;
My daughter will I question how she loves you,
And as I find her, so am I affected.
Till then, farewell, sir: she must needs go in;
Her father will be angry.

FENTON — Farewell, gentle mistress. Farewell, Nan.

[*Exeunt* MRS. PAGE *and* ANNE.]

QUICKLY — This is my doing now: "Nay," said I, "will you cast away your child on a fool, and a physician? Look on Master Fenton." This is my doing.

FENTON — I thank thee; and I pray thee, once to-night
Give my sweet Nan this ring. There's for thy pains.

QUICKLY — Now Heaven send thee good fortune!

[*Exit* FENTON.]

A kind heart he hath; a woman would run through fire and water for such a kind heart. But yet I would my master had Mistress Anne; or I would Master Slender had her; or, in sooth, I would Master Fenton had her; I will do what I can for them all three, for so I have promised, and I'll be as good as my word; but speciously for Master Fenton. Well, I must of another errand to Sir John Falstaff from my two mistresses: what a beast am I to slack it!

[*Exit.*]

SCENE-V — A room in the Garter Inn

[*Enter* FALSTAFF *and* BARDOLPH.]

FALSTAFF Bardolph, I say, —

BARDOLPH Here, sir.

FALSTAFF Go fetch me a quart of sack; put a toast in 't.

[*Exit* BARDOLPH.]

Have I lived to be carried in a basket, and to be thrown in the Thames like a barrow of butcher's offal? Well, if I be served such another trick, I'll have my brains ta'en out and buttered, and give them to a dog for a new year's gift. The rogues slighted me into the river with as little remorse as they would have drowned a blind bitch's puppies, fifteen i' the litter; and you may know by my size that I have a kind of alacrity in sinking; if the bottom were as deep as hell I should down. I had been drowned but that the shore was shelvy and shallow; a death that I abhor, for the water swells a man; and what a thing should I have been when had been swelled! I should have been a mountain of mummy.

[*Re-enter* BARDOLPH, *with the sack.*]

BARDOLPH Here's Mistress Quickly, sir, to speak with you.

FALSTAFF Come, let me pour in some sack to the Thames water; for my belly's as cold as if I had swallowed snowballs for pills to cool the reins. Call her in.

BARDOLPH Come in, woman.

[*Enter* MISTRESS QUICKLY.]

QUICKLY By your leave. I cry you mercy. Give your worship good morrow.

FALSTAFF Take away these chalices. Go, brew me a pottle of sack finely.

BARDOLPH With eggs, sir?

FALSTAFF Simple of itself; I'll no pullet-sperm in my brewage.

[*Exit* BARDOLPH.]

How now!

QUICKLY Marry, sir, I come to your worship from Mistress Ford.

FALSTAFF Mistress Ford! I have had ford enough; I was thrown into the ford; I have my belly full of ford.

QUICKLY Alas the day! good heart, that was not her fault: she does so take on with her men; they mistook their erection.

FALSTAFF So did I mine, to build upon a foolish woman's promise.

QUICKLY Well, she laments, sir, for it, that it would yearn your heart to see it. Her husband goes this morning a-birding; she desires you once more to come to her between eight and nine; I must carry her word quickly. She'll make you amends, I warrant you.

FALSTAFF Well, I will visit her. Tell her so; and bid her think what a man is; let her consider his frailty, and then judge of my merit.

QUICKLY I will tell her.

FALSTAFF Do so. Between nine and ten, sayest thou?

QUICKLY Eight and nine, sir.

FALSTAFF Well, be gone; I will not miss her.

QUICKLY Peace be with you, sir.

[*Exit* MISTRESS QUICKLY.]

FALSTAFF I marvel I hear not of Master Brook; he sent me word to stay within. I like his money well. O! here he comes.

[*Enter* FORD *disguised.*]

FORD Bless you, sir!

FALSTAFF Now, Master Brook, you come to know what hath passed between me and Ford's wife?

FORD That, indeed, Sir John, is my business.

FALSTAFF Master Brook, I will not lie to you: I was at her house the hour she appointed me.

FORD And how sped you, sir?

FALSTAFF Very ill-favouredly, Master Brook.

FORD How so, sir? did she change her determination?

FALSTAFF No. Master Brook; but the peaking cornuto her husband, Master Brook, dwelling in a continual 'larum of jealousy, comes me in the instant of our encounter, after we had embraced, kissed, protested, and, as it were, spoke the prologue of our comedy; and at his heels a rabble of his companions, thither provoked and instigated by his distemper, and, forsooth, to search his house for his wife's love.

FORD What! while you were there?

FALSTAFF While I was there.

FORD And did he search for you, and could not find you?

FALSTAFF You shall hear. As good luck would have it, comes in one Mistress Page; gives intelligence of Ford's approach; and, in her invention and Ford's wife's distraction, they conveyed me into a buck-basket.

FORD A buck-basket!

FALSTAFF By the Lord, a buck-basket! rammed me in with foul shirts and smocks, socks, foul stockings, greasy napkins, that, Master Brook, there was the rankest compound of villainous smell that ever offended nostril.

FORD And how long lay you there?

FALSTAFF Nay, you shall hear, Master Brook, what I have suffered to bring this woman to evil for your good. Being thus crammed in the basket, a couple of Ford's knaves, his hinds, were called forth by their mistress to carry me in the name of foul clothes to Datchet-lane; they took me on their shoulders; met the jealous knave their master in the door; who asked them once or twice what they had in their basket. I quaked for fear lest the lunatic knave would have searched it; but Fate, ordaining he should be a cuckold, held his hand. Well, on went he for a search, and away went I for foul clothes. But mark the sequel, Master Brook: I suffered the pangs of three several deaths: first, an intolerable fright to be detected with a jealous rotten bell-wether; next, to be compassed like a good bilbo in the circumference of a peck, hilt to point, heel to head;

and then, to be stopped in, like a strong distillation, with stinking clothes that fretted in their own grease: think of that; a man of my kidney, think of that, that am as subject to heat as butter; a man of continual dissolution and thaw: it was a miracle to 'scape suffocation. And in the height of this bath, when I was more than half stewed in grease, like a Dutch dish, to be thrown into the Thames, and cooled, glowing hot, in that surge, like a horse-shoe; think of that, hissing hot, think of that, Master Brook!

FORD In good sadness, sir, I am sorry that for my sake you have suffered all this. My suit, then, is desperate; you'll undertake her no more.

FALSTAFF Master Brook, I will be thrown into Etna, as I have been into Thames, ere I will leave her thus. Her husband is this morning gone a-birding; I have received from her another embassy of meeting; 'twixt eight and nine is the hour, Master Brook.

FORD 'Tis past eight already, sir.

FALSTAFF Is it? I will then address me to my appointment. Come to me at your convenient leisure, and you shall know how I speed, and the conclusion shall be crowned with your enjoying her: adieu. You shall have her, Master Brook; Master Brook, you shall cuckold Ford.

[*Exit* FALSTAFF.]

FORD Hum! ha! Is this a vision? Is this a dream? Do I sleep? Master Ford, awake; awake, Master Ford. There's a hole made in your best coat, Master Ford. This 'tis to be married; this 'tis to have linen and buck-baskets! Well, I will proclaim myself what I am; I will now take the lecher; he is at my house. He cannot scape me; 'tis impossible he should; he cannot creep into a half-penny purse, nor into a pepper box; but, lest the devil that guides him should aid him, I will search impossible places. Though what I am I cannot avoid, yet to be what I would not, shall not make me tame; if I have horns to make one mad, let the proverb go with me; I'll be horn-mad.

[*Exit.*]

ACT-IV
SCENE-I — The street

[*Enter* MISTRESS PAGE, MISTRESS QUICKLY, *and* WILLIAM.]

MRS. PAGE	Is he at Master Ford's already, think'st thou?

QUICKLY	Sure he is by this; or will be presently; but truly he is very courageous mad about his throwing into the water. Mistress Ford desires you to come suddenly.

MRS. PAGE	I'll be with her by and by; I'll but bring my young man here to school. Look where his master comes; 'tis a playing day, I see.

[*Enter* SIR HUGH EVANS.]

How now, Sir Hugh, no school to-day?

EVANS	No; Master Slender is let the boys leave to play

QUICKLY	Blessing of his heart!

MRS. PAGE	Sir Hugh, my husband says my son profits nothing in the world at his book; I pray you ask him some questions in his accidence.

EVANS	Come hither, William; hold up your head; come.

MRS. PAGE	Come on, sirrah; hold up your head; answer your master; be not afraid.

EVANS	William, how many numbers is in nouns?

WILLIAM	Two.

QUICKLY	Truly, I thought there had been one number more, because they say "Od's nouns."

EVANS	Peace your tattlings! What is "fair," William?

WILLIAM	Pulcher.

QUICKLY	Polecats! There are fairer things than polecats, sure

EVANS	You are a very simplicity 'oman; I pray you, peace. What is "lapis," William?

WILLIAM A stone.

EVANS And what is "a stone," William?

WILLIAM A pebble.

EVANS No, it is "lapis"; I pray you remember in your prain

WILLIAM Lapis.

EVANS That is a good William. What is he, William, that does lend articles?

WILLIAM Articles are borrowed of the pronoun, and be thus declined: Singulariter, nominativo; hic, haec, hoc.

EVANS Nominativo, hig, hag, hog; pray you, mark: genitivo, hujus. Well, what is your accusative case?

WILLIAM Accusativo, hinc.

EVANS I pray you, have your remembrance, child. Accusativo, hung, hang, hog.

QUICKLY "Hang-hog" is Latin for bacon, I warrant you.

EVANS Leave your prabbles, 'oman. What is the focative case, William?

WILLIAM O vocativo, O.

EVANS Remember, William: focative is caret.

QUICKLY And that's a good root.

EVANS 'Oman, forbear.

MRS. PAGE Peace.

EVANS What is your genitive case plural, William?

WILLIAM Genitive case?

EVANS Ay.

WILLIAM Genitive: horum, harum, horum.

QUICKLY Vengeance of Jenny's case; fie on her! Never name her, child, if she be a whore.

EVANS For shame, 'oman.

QUICKLY You do ill to teach the child such words. He teaches him to hick and to hack, which they'll do fast enough of themselves; and to call "horum;" fie upon you!

EVANS 'Oman, art thou lunatics? Hast thou no understandings for thy cases, and the numbers of the genders? Thou art as foolish Christian creatures as I would desires.

MRS. PAGE Prithee, hold thy peace.

EVANS Show me now, William, some declensions of your pronouns.

WILLIAM Forsooth, I have forgot.

EVANS It is qui, quae, quod; if you forget your "quis", your "quaes", and your "quods", you must be preeches. Go your ways and play; go.

MRS. PAGE He is a better scholar than I thought he was.

EVANS He is a good sprag memory. Farewell, Mistress Page.

MRS. PAGE Adieu, good Sir Hugh.

[*Exit* SIR HUGH.]

Get you home, boy. Come, we stay too long.

[*Exeunt.*]

SCENE-II — A room in Ford's house

[*Enter* FALSTAFF *and* MISTRESS FORD.]

FALSTAFF Mistress Ford, your sorrow hath eaten up my sufferance. I see you are obsequious in your love, and I profess requital to a hair's breadth; not only, Mistress Ford, in the simple office of love, but in all the accoutrement, complement, and ceremony of it. But are you sure of your husband now?

MRS. FORD He's a-birding, sweet Sir John.

MRS. PAGE [*Within*] What ho! gossip Ford, what ho!

MRS. FORD Step into the chamber, Sir John.

[*Exit* FALSTAFF.]

[*Enter* MISTRESS PAGE.]

MRS. PAGE How now, sweetheart! who's at home besides yourself?

MRS. FORD Why, none but mine own people.

MRS. PAGE Indeed!

MRS. FORD No, certainly. —
[*Aside to her*] Speak louder.

MRS. PAGE Truly, I am so glad you have nobody here.

MRS. FORD Why?

MRS. PAGE Why, woman, your husband is in his old lunes again. He so takes on yonder with my husband; so rails against all married mankind; so curses all Eve's daughters, of what complexion soever; and so buffets himself on the forehead, crying "Peer out, peer out!" that any madness I ever yet beheld seemed but tameness, civility, and patience, to this his distemper he is in now. I am glad the fat knight is not here.

MRS. FORD Why, does he talk of him?

MRS. PAGE Of none but him; and swears he was carried out, the last time he searched for him, in a basket; protests to my husband he is now here; and hath drawn him and the rest of their company from their sport, to make another experiment of his suspicion. But I am glad the knight is not here; now he shall see his own foolery.

MRS. FORD How near is he, Mistress Page?

MRS. PAGE Hard by, at street end; he will be here anon.

MRS. FORD I am undone! the knight is here.

MRS. PAGE Why, then, you are utterly shamed, and he's but a dead man. What a woman are you! Away with him, away with him! better shame than murder.

MRS. FORD Which way should he go? How should I bestow him? Shall I put him into the basket again?

[*Re-enter* FALSTAFF.]

FALSTAFF No, I'll come no more i' the basket. May I not go out ere he come?

MRS. PAGE Alas! three of Master Ford's brothers watch the door with pistols, that none shall issue out; otherwise you might slip away ere he came. But what make you here?

FALSTAFF What shall I do? I'll creep up into the chimney.

MRS. FORD There they always use to discharge their birding-pieces.

MRS. PAGE Creep into the kiln-hole.

FALSTAFF Where is it?

MRS. FORD He will seek there, on my word. Neither press, coffer, chest, trunk, well, vault, but he hath an abstract for the remembrance of such places, and goes to them by his note: there is no hiding you in the house.

FALSTAFF I'll go out then.

MRS. PAGE If you go out in your own semblance, you die, Sir John. Unless you go out disguised, —

MRS. FORD How might we disguise him?

MRS. PAGE Alas the day! I know not! There is no woman's gown big enough for him; otherwise he might put on a hat, a muffler, and a kerchief, and so escape.

FALSTAFF Good hearts, devise something: any extremity rather than a mischief.

MRS. FORD My maid's aunt, the fat woman of Brainford, has a gown above.

MRS. PAGE On my word, it will serve him; she's as big as he is; and there's her thrummed hat, and her muffler too. Run up, Sir John.

MRS. FORD Go, go, sweet Sir John. Mistress Page and I will look some linen for your head.

MRS. PAGE Quick, quick! we'll come dress you straight; put on the gown the while.

[*Exit* FALSTAFF.]

MRS. FORD I would my husband would meet him in this shape; he cannot abide the old woman of Brainford; he swears she's a witch, forbade her my house, and hath threatened to beat her.

MRS. PAGE Heaven guide him to thy husband's cudgel; and the devil guide his cudgel afterwards!

MRS. FORD But is my husband coming?

MRS. PAGE Ay, in good sadness is he; and talks of the basket too, howsoever he hath had intelligence.

MRS. FORD We'll try that; for I'll appoint my men to carry the basket again, to meet him at the door with it as they did last time.

MRS. PAGE Nay, but he'll be here presently; let's go dress him like the witch of Brainford.

MRS. FORD I'll first direct my men what they shall do with the basket. Go up; I'll bring linen for him straight.

[*Exit* MISTRESS FORD.]

MRS. PAGE Hang him, dishonest varlet! we cannot misuse him enough.
We'll leave a proof, by that which we will do,
Wives may be merry and yet honest too.
We do not act that often jest and laugh;
'Tis old but true: "Still swine eats all the draff."

[*Exit.*]

[*Re-enter* MISTRESS FORD, *with two* SERVANTS.]

MRS. FORD Go, sirs, take the basket again on your shoulders; your master is hard at door; if he bid you set it down, obey him. Quickly, dispatch.

[*Exit* MISTRESS FORD.]

FIRST SERVANT Come, come, take it up.

SECOND SERVANT Pray heaven, it be not full of knight again.

FIRST SERVANT I hope not; I had lief as bear so much lead.

[*Enter* FORD, PAGE, SHALLOW, CAIUS, *and* SIR HUGH EVANS.]

FORD Ay, but if it prove true, Master Page, have you any way then to unfool me again? Set down the basket, villain! Somebody call my wife. Youth in a basket! O you panderly rascals! there's a knot, a ging, a pack, a conspiracy against me. Now shall the devil be shamed. What, wife, I say! Come, come forth! behold what honest clothes you send forth to bleaching!

PAGE Why, this passes, Master Ford! you are not to go loose any longer; you must be pinioned.

EVANS Why, this is lunatics! this is mad as a mad dog.

SHALLOW Indeed, Master Ford, this is not well, indeed.

FORD So say I too, sir. —

[*Re-enter* MISTRESS FORD.]

Come hither, Mistress Ford, the honest woman, the modest wife, the virtuous creature, that hath the jealous fool to her husband! I suspect without cause, Mistress, do I?

MRS. FORD Heaven be my witness, you do, if you suspect me in any dishonesty.

FORD Well said, brazen-face! hold it out. Come forth, sirrah. [*Pulling clothes out of the basket*]

PAGE This passes!

MRS. FORD Are you not ashamed? Let the clothes alone.

FORD I shall find you anon.

EVANS 'Tis unreasonable. Will you take up your wife's clothes? Come away.

FORD Empty the basket, I say!

MRS. FORD Why, man, why?

FORD Master Page, as I am a man, there was one conveyed out of my house yesterday in this basket: why may not he be

	there again? In my house I am sure he is; my intelligence is true; my jealousy is reasonable. Pluck me out all the linen.
MRS. FORD	If you find a man there, he shall die a flea's death.
PAGE	Here's no man.
SHALLOW	By my fidelity, this is not well, Master Ford; this wrongs you.
EVANS	Master Ford, you must pray, and not follow the imaginations of your own heart; this is jealousies.
FORD	Well, he's not here I seek for.
PAGE	No, nor nowhere else but in your brain.

[*Servants carry away the basket.*]

FORD	Help to search my house this one time. If I find not what I seek, show no colour for my extremity; let me for ever be your table-sport; let them say of me "As jealous as Ford, that searched a hollow walnut for his wife's leman." Satisfy me once more; once more search with me.
MRS. FORD	What, hoa, Mistress Page! Come you and the old woman down; my husband will come into the chamber.
FORD	Old woman? what old woman's that?
MRS. FORD	Why, it is my maid's aunt of Brainford.
FORD	A witch, a quean, an old cozening quean! Have I not forbid her my house? She comes of errands, does she? We are simple men; we do not know what's brought to pass under the profession of fortune-telling. She works by charms, by spells, by the figure, and such daubery as this is, beyond our element. We know nothing. Come down, you witch, you hag you; come down, I say!
MRS. FORD	Nay, good sweet husband! Good gentlemen, let him not strike the old woman.

[*Re-enter* FALSTAFF *in woman's clothes, led by* MISTRESS PAGE.]

MRS. PAGE	Come, Mother Prat; come, give me your hand.
FORD	I'll prat her. — [*Beats him.*] Out of my door, you witch, you rag, you baggage, you polecat, you ronyon! Out, out! I'll conjure you, I'll fortune-tell you.

[*Exit* FALSTAFF.]

MRS. PAGE Are you not ashamed? I think you have killed the poor woman.

MRS. FORD Nay, he will do it. 'Tis a goodly credit for you.

FORD Hang her, witch!

EVANS By yea and no, I think the 'oman is a witch indeed; I like not when a 'oman has a great peard; I spy a great peard under her muffler.

FORD Will you follow, gentlemen? I beseech you follow; see but the issue of my jealousy; if I cry out thus upon no trail, never trust me when I open again.

PAGE Let's obey his humour a little further. Come, gentlemen.

[*Exeunt* FORD, PAGE, SHALLOW, CAIUS, *and* EVANS.]

MRS. PAGE Trust me, he beat him most pitifully.

MRS. FORD Nay, by the mass, that he did not; he beat him most unpitifully methought.

MRS. PAGE I'll have the cudgel hallowed and hung o'er the altar; it hath done meritorious service.

MRS. FORD What think you? May we, with the warrant of womanhood and the witness of a good conscience, pursue him with any further revenge?

MRS. PAGE. The spirit of wantonness is sure scared out of him; if the devil have him not in fee-simple, with fine and recovery, he will never, I think, in the way of waste, attempt us again.

MRS. FORD Shall we tell our husbands how we have served him?

MRS. PAGE Yes, by all means; if it be but to scrape the figures out of your husband's brains. If they can find in their hearts the poor unvirtuous fat knight shall be any further afflicted, we two will still be the ministers.

MRS. FORD I'll warrant they'll have him publicly shamed; and methinks there would be no period to the jest, should he not be publicly shamed.

MRS. PAGE Come, to the forge with it then; shape it. I would not have things cool.

[*Exeunt.*]

SCENE-III — A room in the Garter Inn

[*Enter* HOST *and* BARDOLPH.]

BARDOLPH Sir, the Germans desire to have three of your horses; the Duke himself will be to-morrow at court, and they are going to meet him.

HOST What duke should that be comes so secretly? I hear not of him in the court. Let me speak with the gentlemen; they speak English?

BARDOLPH Ay, sir; I'll call them to you.

HOST They shall have my horses, but I'll make them pay; I'll sauce them; they have had my house a week at command; I have turned away my other guests. They must come off; I'll sauce them. Come.

[*Exeunt.*]

SCENE-IV — A room in Ford's house

[*Enter* PAGE, FORD, MISTRESS PAGE, MISTRESS FORD, *and* SIR HUGH EVANS.]

EVANS 'Tis one of the best discretions of a 'oman as ever I did look upon.

PAGE And did he send you both these letters at an instant?

MRS. PAGE Within a quarter of an hour.

FORD Pardon me, wife. Henceforth, do what thou wilt;
I rather will suspect the sun with cold
Than thee with wantonness: now doth thy honour stand,
In him that was of late an heretic,
As firm as faith.

PAGE 'Tis well, 'tis well; no more.
Be not as extreme in submission
As in offence;
But let our plot go forward: let our wives
Yet once again, to make us public sport,
Appoint a meeting with this old fat fellow,
Where we may take him and disgrace him for it.

FORD There is no better way than that they spoke of.

PAGE How? To send him word they'll meet him in the park at midnight? Fie, fie! he'll never come!

EVANS You say he has been thrown in the rivers; and has been grievously peaten as an old 'oman; methinks there should be terrors in him, that he should not come; methinks his flesh is punished; he shall have no desires.

PAGE So think I too.

MRS. FORD Devise but how you'll use him when he comes,
And let us two devise to bring him thither.

MRS. PAGE There is an old tale goes that Herne the hunter,
Sometime a keeper here in Windsor Forest,
Doth all the winter-time, at still midnight,
Walk round about an oak, with great ragg'd horns;
And there he blasts the tree, and takes the cattle,
And makes milch-kine yield blood, and shakes a chain
In a most hideous and dreadful manner:
You have heard of such a spirit, and well you know
The superstitious idle-headed eld
Received, and did deliver to our age,
This tale of Herne the hunter for a truth.

PAGE Why, yet there want not many that do fear
In deep of night to walk by this Herne's oak.
But what of this?

MRS. FORD Marry, this is our device;
That Falstaff at that oak shall meet with us,
Disguis'd, like Herne, with huge horns on his head.

PAGE Well, let it not be doubted but he'll come,
And in this shape. When you have brought him thither,
What shall be done with him? What is your plot?

MRS. PAGE That likewise have we thought upon, and thus:
Nan Page my daughter, and my little son,
And three or four more of their growth, we'll dress
Like urchins, ouphs, and fairies, green and white,
With rounds of waxen tapers on their heads,
And rattles in their hands. Upon a sudden,
As Falstaff, she, and I, are newly met,
Let them from forth a sawpit rush at once
With some diffusèd song; upon their sight
We two in great amazèdness will fly:
Then let them all encircle him about,
And fairy-like, to pinch the unclean knight;
And ask him why, that hour of fairy revel,
In their so sacred paths he dares to tread
In shape profane.

MRS. FORD And till he tell the truth,
Let the supposèd fairies pinch him sound,
And burn him with their tapers.

MRS. PAGE The truth being known,
We'll all present ourselves; dis-horn the spirit,
And mock him home to Windsor.

FORD The children must
Be practis'd well to this or they'll ne'er do 't.

EVANS I will teach the children their behaviours; and I will be like a jack-an-apes also, to burn the knight with my taber.

FORD That will be excellent. I'll go buy them vizards.

MRS. PAGE My Nan shall be the Queen of all the Fairies,
Finely attired in a robe of white.

PAGE That silk will I go buy.
[*Aside*] And in that time
Shall Master Slender steal my Nan away,
And marry her at Eton. Go, send to Falstaff straight.

FORD Nay, I'll to him again, in name of Brook;
He'll tell me all his purpose. Sure, he'll come.

MRS. PAGE Fear not you that. Go, get us properties
And tricking for our fairies.

EVANS Let us about it. It is admirable pleasures, and fery honest knaveries.

[*Exeunt* PAGE, FORD, *and* EVANS.]

MRS. PAGE Go, Mistress Ford.
Send Quickly to Sir John to know his mind.

[*Exit* MRS. FORD.]

I'll to the Doctor; he hath my good will,
And none but he, to marry with Nan Page.
That Slender, though well landed, is an idiot;
And he my husband best of all affects:
The Doctor is well money'd, and his friends
Potent at court: he, none but he, shall have her,
Though twenty thousand worthier come to crave her.

[*Exit.*]

SCENE-V — A room in the Garter Inn

[*Enter* HOST *and* SIMPLE.]

HOST — What wouldst thou have, boor? What, thick-skin? Speak, breathe, discuss; brief, short, quick, snap.

SIMPLE — Marry, sir, I come to speak with Sir John Falstaff from Master Slender.

HOST — There's his chamber, his house, his castle, his standing-bed and truckle-bed; 'tis painted about with the story of the Prodigal, fresh and new. Go knock and call; he'll speak like an Anthropophaginian unto thee; knock, I say.

SIMPLE — There's an old woman, a fat woman, gone up into his chamber; I'll be so bold as stay, sir, till she come down; I come to speak with her, indeed.

HOST — Ha! a fat woman? The knight may be robbed. I'll call. Bully knight! Bully Sir John! Speak from thy lungs military. Art thou there? It is thine host, thine Ephesian, calls.

FALSTAFF — [*Above*] How now, mine host?

HOST — Here's a Bohemian-Tartar tarries the coming down of thy fat woman. Let her descend, bully, let her descend; my chambers are honourible. Fie! privacy? fie!

[*Enter* FALSTAFF.]

FALSTAFF — There was, mine host, an old fat woman even now with, me; but she's gone.

SIMPLE — Pray you, sir, was't not the wise woman of Brainford?

FALSTAFF — Ay, marry was it, mussel-shell: what would you with her?

SIMPLE — My master, sir, my Master Slender, sent to her, seeing her go thorough the streets, to know, sir, whether one Nym, sir, that beguiled him of a chain, had the chain or no.

FALSTAFF — I spake with the old woman about it.

SIMPLE — And what says she, I pray, sir?

FALSTAFF — Marry, she says that the very same man that beguiled Master Slender of his chain cozened him of it.

SIMPLE — I would I could have spoken with the woman herself; I had other things to have spoken with her too, from him.

FALSTAFF — What are they? Let us know.

HOST — Ay, come; quick.

SIMPLE — I may not conceal them, sir.

FALSTAFF — Conceal them, or thou diest.

SIMPLE — Why, sir, they were nothing but about Mistress Anne Page: to know if it were my master's fortune to have her or no.

FALSTAFF — 'Tis, 'tis his fortune.

SIMPLE — What sir?

FALSTAFF — To have her, or no. Go; say the woman told me so.

SIMPLE — May I be bold to say so, sir?

FALSTAFF — Ay, Sir Tike; like who more bold?

SIMPLE — I thank your worship; I shall make my master glad with these tidings.

[*Exit* SIMPLE.]

HOST — Thou art clerkly, thou art clerkly, Sir John. Was there a wise woman with thee?

FALSTAFF — Ay, that there was, mine host; one that hath taught me more wit than ever I learned before in my life; and I paid nothing for it neither, but was paid for my learning.

[*Enter* BARDOLPH.]

BARDOLPH — Out, alas, sir! cozenage, mere cozenage!

HOST — Where be my horses? Speak well of them, varletto.

BARDOLPH — Run away, with the cozeners; for so soon as I came beyond Eton, they threw me off, from behind one of them, in a slough of mire; and set spurs and away, like three German devils, three Doctor Faustuses.

HOST They are gone but to meet the Duke, villain; do not say they be fled; Germans are honest men.

[*Enter* SIR HUGH EVANS.]

EVANS Where is mine host?

HOST What is the matter, sir?

EVANS Have a care of your entertainments: there is a friend of mine come to town tells me there is three cozen-germans that has cozened all the hosts of Readins, of Maidenhead, of Colebrook, of horses and money. I tell you for good will, look you; you are wise, and full of gibes and vlouting-stogs, and 'tis not convenient you should be cozened. Fare you well.

[*Exit* EVANS.]

[*Enter* DOCTOR CAIUS.]

CAIUS Vere is mine host de Jarteer?

HOST Here, Master Doctor, in perplexity and doubtful dilemma.

CAIUS I cannot tell vat is dat; but it is tell-a me dat you make grand preparation for a Duke de Jamany. By my trot, dere is no duke that the court is know to come; I tell you for good will: Adieu.

[*Exit* DOCTOR CAIUS.]

HOST Hue and cry, villain, go! Assist me, knight; I am undone. Fly, run, hue and cry, villain; I am undone!

[*Exeunt* HOST *and* BARDOLPH.]

FALSTAFF I would all the world might be cozened, for I have been cozened and beaten too. If it should come to the ear of the court how I have been transformed, and how my transformation hath been washed and cudgelled, they would melt me out of my fat, drop by drop, and liquor fishermen's boots with me; I warrant they would whip me with their fine wits till I were as crest-fallen as a dried pear. I never prospered since I forswore myself at primero. Well, if my wind were but long enough to say my prayers, I would repent.

[*Enter* MISTRESS QUICKLY.]

Now! whence come you?

QUICKLY From the two parties, forsooth.

FALSTAFF The devil take one party and his dam the other! And so they shall be both bestowed. I have suffered more for their sakes, more than the villainous inconstancy of man's disposition is able to bear.

QUICKLY And have not they suffered? Yes, I warrant; speciously one of them; Mistress Ford, good heart, is beaten black and blue, that you cannot see a white spot about her.

FALSTAFF What tellest thou me of black and blue? I was beaten myself into all the colours of the rainbow; and was like to be apprehended for the witch of Brainford. But that my admirable dexterity of wit, my counterfeiting the action of an old woman, delivered me, the knave constable had set me i' the stocks, i' the common stocks, for a witch.

QUICKLY Sir, let me speak with you in your chamber; you shall hear how things go, and, I warrant, to your content. Here is a letter will say somewhat. Good hearts, what ado here is to bring you together! Sure, one of you does not serve heaven well, that you are so crossed.

FALSTAFF Come up into my chamber.

[*Exeunt*.]

SCENE-VI — Another room in the Garter Inn

[*Enter* FENTON *and* HOST.]

HOST — Master Fenton, talk not to me; my mind is heavy; I will give over all.

FENTON — Yet hear me speak. Assist me in my purpose,
And, as I am a gentleman, I'll give thee
A hundred pound in gold more than your loss.

HOST — I will hear you, Master Fenton; and I will, at the least, keep your counsel.

FENTON — From time to time I have acquainted you
With the dear love I bear to fair Anne Page,
Who, mutually, hath answered my affection,
So far forth as herself might be her chooser,
Even to my wish. I have a letter from her
Of such contents as you will wonder at;
The mirth whereof so larded with my matter
That neither, singly, can be manifested
Without the show of both; wherein fat Falstaff
Hath a great scare: the image of the jest
I'll show you here at large. Hark, good mine host:
To-night at Herne's oak, just 'twixt twelve and one,
Must my sweet Nan present the Fairy Queen;
The purpose why is here: in which disguise,
While other jests are something rank on foot,
Her father hath commanded her to slip
Away with Slender, and with him at Eton
Immediately to marry; she hath consented:
Now, sir,
Her mother, even strong against that match
And firm for Doctor Caius, hath appointed

That he shall likewise shuffle her away,
While other sports are tasking of their minds;
And at the deanery, where a priest attends,
Straight marry her: to this her mother's plot
She seemingly obedient likewise hath
Made promise to the doctor. Now thus it rests:
Her father means she shall be all in white;
And in that habit, when Slender sees his time
To take her by the hand and bid her go,
She shall go with him: her mother hath intended
The better to denote her to the doctor, —
For they must all be mask'd and vizarded —
That quaint in green she shall be loose enrob'd,
With ribands pendent, flaring 'bout her head;
And when the doctor spies his vantage ripe,
To pinch her by the hand: and, on that token,
The maid hath given consent to go with him.

HOST Which means she to deceive, father or mother?

FENTON Both, my good host, to go along with me:
And here it rests, that you'll procure the vicar
To stay for me at church, 'twixt twelve and one,
And in the lawful name of marrying,
To give our hearts united ceremony.

HOST Well, husband your device; I'll to the vicar.
Bring you the maid, you shall not lack a priest.

FENTON So shall I evermore be bound to thee;
Besides, I'll make a present recompense.

[*Exeunt.*]

ACT-V

SCENE-I — A room in the Garter Inn

[*Enter* FALSTAFF *and* MISTRESS QUICKLY.]

FALSTAFF Prithee, no more prattling; go: I'll hold. This is the third time; I hope good luck lies in odd numbers. Away! go. They say there is divinity in odd numbers, either in nativity, chance, or death. Away!

QUICKLY I'll provide you a chain, and I'll do what I can to get you a pair of horns.

FALSTAFF Away, I say; time wears; hold up your head, and mince.

[*Exit* MRS. QUICKLY.]

[*Enter* FORD.]

How now, Master Brook! Master Brook, the matter will be known tonight, or never. Be you in the Park about midnight, at Herne's oak, and you shall see wonders.

FORD Went you not to her yesterday, sir, as you told me you had appointed?

FALSTAFF I went to her, Master Brook, as you see, like a poor old man; but I came from her, Master Brook, like a poor old woman. That same knave Ford, her husband, hath the finest mad devil of jealousy in him, Master Brook, that ever governed frenzy. I will tell you: he beat me grievously in the shape of a woman; for in the shape of man, Master Brook, I fear not Goliath with a weaver's beam, because I know also life is a shuttle. I am in haste; go along with me; I'll tell you all, Master Brook. Since I plucked geese, played truant, and whipped top, I knew not what 'twas to be beaten till lately. Follow me: I'll tell you strange things of this knave Ford, on whom to-night I will be revenged, and I will deliver his wife into your hand. Follow. Strange things in hand, Master Brook! Follow.

[*Exeunt.*]

SCENE-II — Windsor Park

[*Enter* PAGE, SHALLOW, *and* SLENDER.]

PAGE Come, come; we'll couch i' the castle-ditch till we see the light of our fairies. Remember, son Slender, my daughter.

SLENDER Ay, forsooth; I have spoke with her, and we have a nay-word how to know one another. I come to her in white and cry "mum"; she cries "budget," and by that we know one another.

SHALLOW That's good too; but what needs either your "mum" or her "budget"? The white will decipher her well enough. It hath struck ten o'clock.

PAGE The night is dark; light and spirits will become it well. Heaven prosper our sport! No man means evil but the devil, and we shall know him by his horns. Let's away; follow me.

[*Exeunt.*]

SCENE-III — The street in Windsor

[*Enter* MISTRESS PAGE, MISTRESS FORD, *and* DOCTOR CAIUS.]

MRS. PAGE Master Doctor, my daughter is in green; when you see your time, take her by the hand, away with her to the deanery, and dispatch it quickly. Go before into the Park; we two must go together.

CAIUS I know vat I have to do; adieu.

MRS. PAGE Fare you well, sir.

[*Exit* CAIUS.]

My husband will not rejoice so much at the abuse of Falstaff as he will chafe at the doctor's marrying my daughter; but 'tis no matter; better a little chiding than a great deal of heart break.

MRS. FORD Where is Nan now, and her troop of fairies, and the Welsh devil, Hugh?

MRS. PAGE They are all couched in a pit hard by Herne's oak, with obscured lights; which, at the very instant of Falstaff's and our meeting, they will at once display to the night.

MRS. FORD That cannot choose but amaze him.

MRS. PAGE If he be not amazed, he will be mocked; if he be amazed, he will every way be mocked.

MRS. FORD We'll betray him finely.

MRS. PAGE Against such lewdsters and their lechery,
Those that betray them do no treachery.

MRS. FORD The hour draws on: to the oak, to the oak!

[*Exeunt.*]

SCENE-IV — Windsor Park

[*Enter* SIR HUGH EVANS, *disguised, with others as Fairies.*]

EVANS Trib, trib, fairies; come; and remember your parts. Be pold, I pray you; follow me into the pit; and when I give the watch-ords, do as I pid you. Come, come; trib, trib.

[*Exeunt.*]

SCENE-V — Another part of the Park

[*Enter* FALSTAFF *disguised as* HERNE *with a buck's head on.*]

FALSTAFF The Windsor bell hath struck twelve; the minute draws on. Now the hot-blooded gods assist me! Remember, Jove, thou wast a bull for thy Europa; love set on thy horns. O powerful love! that in some respects, makes a beast a man; in some other a man a beast. You were also, Jupiter, a swan, for the love of Leda. O omnipotent love! how near the god drew to the complexion of a goose! A fault done first in the form of a beast; O Jove, a beastly fault! and then another fault in the semblance of a fowl: think on't, Jove, a foul fault! When gods have hot backs what shall poor men do? For me, I am here a Windsor stag; and the fattest, I think, i' the forest. Send me a cool rut-time, Jove, or who can blame me to piss my tallow? Who comes here? my doe?

[*Enter* MISTRESS FORD *and* MISTRESS PAGE.]

MRS. FORD Sir John! Art thou there, my deer? my male deer?

FALSTAFF My doe with the black scut! Let the sky rain potatoes; let it thunder to the tune of "Greensleeves"; hail kissing-comfits and snow eringoes; let there come a tempest of provocation, I will shelter me here.

[*Embracing her*]

MRS. FORD Mistress Page is come with me, sweetheart.

FALSTAFF Divide me like a brib'd buck, each a haunch; I will keep my sides to myself, my shoulders for the fellow of this walk, and my horns I bequeath your husbands. Am I a woodman, ha? Speak I like Herne the hunter? Why, now is Cupid a child of conscience; he makes restitution. As I am a true spirit, welcome!

[*Noise within*]

MRS. PAGE Alas! what noise?

MRS. FORD Heaven forgive our sins!

FALSTAFF What should this be?

MRS. FORD Away, away!

MRS. PAGE Away, away!

[*They run off.*]

FALSTAFF I think the devil will not have me damned, lest the oil that's in me should set hell on fire; he would never else cross me thus.

[*Enter* SIR HUGH EVANS *like a Satyr,* PISTOL *as a Hobgoblin,* ANNE PAGE *as the the Fairy Queen, attended by her Brothers and Others, as fairies, with waxen tapers on their heads.*]

ANNE Fairies, black, grey, green, and white,
You moonshine revellers, and shades of night,
You orphan heirs of fixèd destiny,
Attend your office and your quality.
Crier Hobgoblin, make the fairy oyes.

PISTOL Elves, list your names: silence, you airy toys!
Cricket, to Windsor chimneys shalt thou leap:
Where fires thou find'st unrak'd, and hearths unswept,
There pinch the maids as blue as bilberry:
Our radiant Queen hates sluts and sluttery.

FALSTAFF They are fairies; he that speaks to them shall die:
I'll wink and couch: no man their works must eye.

[*Lies down upon his face.*]

EVANS Where's Bede? Go you, and where you find a maid
That, ere she sleep, has thrice her prayers said,
Rein up the organs of her fantasy,
Sleep she as sound as careless infancy;
But those as sleep and think not on their sins,
Pinch them, arms, legs, backs, shoulders, sides, and shins.

ANNE About, about!
Search Windsor castle, elves, within and out:
Strew good luck, ouphes, on every sacred room,

That it may stand till the perpetual doom,
In state as wholesome as in state 'tis fit,
Worthy the owner and the owner it.
The several chairs of order look you scour
With juice of balm and every precious flower:
Each fair instalment, coat, and several crest,
With loyal blazon, evermore be blest!
And nightly, meadow-fairies, look you sing,
Like to the Garter's compass, in a ring:
The expressure that it bears, green let it be,
More fertile-fresh than all the field to see;
And "Honi soit qui mal y pense" write
In emerald tufts, flowers purple, blue and white;
Like sapphire, pearl, and rich embroidery,
Buckled below fair knighthood's bending knee.
Fairies use flowers for their charactery.
Away! disperse! But, till 'tis one o'clock,
Our dance of custom round about the oak
Of Herne the hunter let us not forget.

EVANS Pray you, lock hand in hand; yourselves in order set;
And twenty glow-worms shall our lanterns be,
To guide our measure round about the tree.
But, stay; I smell a man of middle-earth.

FALSTAFF Heavens defend me from that Welsh fairy, lest he transform me to a piece of cheese!

PISTOL Vile worm, thou wast o'erlook'd even in thy birth.

ANNE With trial-fire touch me his finger-end:
If he be chaste, the flame will back descend
And turn him to no pain; but if he start,
It is the flesh of a corrupted heart.

PISTOL A trial! come.

EVANS Come, will this wood take fire?

[*They burn him with their tapers.*]

FALSTAFF Oh, oh, oh!

ANNE Corrupt, corrupt, and tainted in desire!
About him, fairies; sing a scornful rhyme;
And, as you trip, still pinch him to your time.

SONG.

Fie on sinful fantasy!
Fie on lust and luxury!
Lust is but a bloody fire,
Kindled with unchaste desire,
Fed in heart, whose flames aspire,
As thoughts do blow them, higher and higher.
Pinch him, fairies, mutually;
Pinch him for his villany;
Pinch him and burn him and turn him about,
Till candles and star-light and moonshine be out.

[*During this song the Fairies pinch* FALSTAFF. DOCTOR CAIUS *comes one way, and steals away a fairy in green; SLENDER another way, and takes off a fairy in white; and* FENTON *comes, and steals away* ANNE PAGE. *A noise of hunting is heard within. All the fairies run away.* FALSTAFF *pulls off his buck's head, and rises*.]

[*Enter* PAGE, FORD, MISTRESS PAGE, MISTRESS FORD. *They lay hold on* FALSTAFF.]

PAGE Nay, do not fly; I think we have watch'd you now:
Will none but Herne the hunter serve your turn?

MRS. PAGE I pray you, come, hold up the jest no higher.
Now, good Sir John, how like you Windsor wives?
See you these, husband? do not these fair yokes
Become the forest better than the town?

FORD Now, sir, who's a cuckold now? Master Brook, Falstaff's a knave, a cuckoldly knave; here are his horns, Master Brook; and, Master Brook, he hath enjoyed nothing of Ford's but his buck-basket, his cudgel, and twenty pounds of money, which must be paid to Master Brook; his horses are arrested for it, Master Brook.

MRS. FORD Sir John, we have had ill luck; we could never meet. I will never take you for my love again; but I will always count you my deer.

FALSTAFF I do begin to perceive that I am made an ass.

FORD Ay, and an ox too; both the proofs are extant.

FALSTAFF And these are not fairies? I was three or four times in the thought they were not fairies; and yet the guiltiness of my mind, the sudden surprise of my powers, drove the grossness of the foppery into a received belief, in despite of the teeth of all rhyme and reason, that they were fairies. See now how wit may be made a Jack-a-Lent when 'tis upon ill employment!

EVANS Sir John Falstaff, serve Got, and leave your desires, and fairies will not pinse you.

FORD Well said, fairy Hugh.

EVANS And leave you your jealousies too, I pray you.

FORD I will never mistrust my wife again, till thou art able to woo her in good English.

FALSTAFF Have I laid my brain in the sun, and dried it, that it wants matter to prevent so gross o'er-reaching as this? Am I ridden with a Welsh goat too? Shall I have a cox-comb of frieze? 'Tis time I were choked with a piece of toasted cheese.

EVANS Seese is not good to give putter: your belly is all putter.

FALSTAFF "Seese" and "putter"! Have I lived to stand at the taunt of one that makes fritters of English? This is enough to be the decay of lust and late-walking through the realm.

MRS. PAGE Why, Sir John, do you think, though we would have thrust virtue out of our hearts by the head and shoulders, and have given ourselves without scruple to hell, that ever the devil could have made you our delight?

FORD What, a hodge-pudding? a bag of flax?

MRS. PAGE A puffed man?

PAGE Old, cold, withered, and of intolerable entrails?

FORD And one that is as slanderous as Satan?

PAGE And as poor as Job?

FORD And as wicked as his wife?

EVANS And given to fornications, and to taverns, and sack and wine, and metheglins, and to drinkings and swearings and starings, pribbles and prabbles?

FALSTAFF Well, I am your theme; you have the start of me; I am dejected; I am not able to answer the Welsh flannel.

Ignorance itself is a plummet o'er me; use me as you will.

FORD Marry, sir, we'll bring you to Windsor, to one Master Brook, that you have cozened of money, to whom you should have been a pander: over and above that you have suffered, I think to repay that money will be a biting affliction.

MRS. FORD Nay, husband, let that go to make amends;
Forget that sum, so we'll all be friends.

FORD Well, here's my hand: all is forgiven at last.

PAGE Yet be cheerful, knight; thou shalt eat a posset tonight at my house; where I will desire thee to laugh at my wife, that now laughs at thee. Tell her, Master Slender hath married her daughter.

MRS. PAGE [*Aside*] Doctors doubt that; if Anne Page be my daughter, she is, by this, Doctor Caius' wife.

[*Enter* SLENDER.]

SLENDER Whoa, ho! ho! father Page!

PAGE Son, how now! how now, son! have you dispatched?

SLENDER Dispatched! I'll make the best in Gloucestershire know on't; would I were hanged, la, else!

PAGE Of what, son?

SLENDER I came yonder at Eton to marry Mistress Anne Page, and she's a great lubberly boy: if it had not been i' the church, I would have swinged him, or he should have swinged me. If I did not think it had been Anne Page, would I might never stir! and 'tis a postmaster's boy.

PAGE Upon my life, then, you took the wrong.

SLENDER What need you tell me that? I think so, when I took a boy for a girl. If I had been married to him, for all he was in woman's apparel, I would not have had him.

PAGE Why, this is your own folly. Did not I tell you how you should know my daughter by her garments?

SLENDER I went to her in white and cried "mum" and she cried "budget" as Anne and I had appointed; and yet it was not Anne, but a postmaster's boy.

EVANS — Jeshu! Master Slender, cannot you see put marry poys?

PAGE — O I am vexed at heart: what shall I do?

MRS. PAGE — Good George, be not angry: I knew of your purpose; turned my daughter into green; and, indeed, she is now with the doctor at the deanery, and there married.

[*Enter* DOCTOR CAIUS.]

CAIUS — Vere is Mistress Page? By gar, I am cozened; I ha' married un garçon, a boy; un paysan, by gar, a boy; it is not Anne Page; by gar, I am cozened.

MRS. PAGE — Why, did you take her in green?

CAIUS — Ay, by gar, and 'tis a boy: by gar, I'll raise all Windsor.

[*Exit* DOCTOR CAIUS.]

FORD — This is strange. Who hath got the right Anne?

PAGE — My heart misgives me; here comes Master Fenton.

[*Enter* FENTON *and* ANNE PAGE.]

How now, Master Fenton!

ANNE — Pardon, good father! good my mother, pardon!

PAGE — Now, Mistress, how chance you went not with Master Slender?

MRS. PAGE — Why went you not with Master Doctor, maid?

FENTON — You do amaze her: hear the truth of it.
You would have married her most shamefully,
Where there was no proportion held in love.
The truth is, she and I, long since contracted,
Are now so sure that nothing can dissolve us.
The offence is holy that she hath committed,
And this deceit loses the name of craft,
Of disobedience, or unduteous title,
Since therein she doth evitate and shun
A thousand irreligious cursèd hours,
Which forcèd marriage would have brought upon her.

FORD — Stand not amaz'd: here is no remedy:
In love, the heavens themselves do guide the state:
Money buys lands, and wives are sold by fate.

FALSTAFF — I am glad, though you have ta'en a special stand to strike at me, that your arrow hath glanced.

PAGE — Well, what remedy? — Fenton, heaven give thee joy!
What cannot be eschew'd must be embrac'd.

FALSTAFF — When night-dogs run, all sorts of deer are chas'd.

MRS. PAGE — Well, I will muse no further. Master Fenton,
Heaven give you many, many merry days!
Good husband, let us every one go home,
And laugh this sport o'er by a country fire;
Sir John and all.

FORD — Let it be so. Sir John,
To Master Brook you yet shall hold your word;
For he, to-night, shall lie with Mistress Ford.

[*Exeunt.*]

* * *

www.ingramcontent.com/pod-product-compliance
Lightning Source LLC
LaVergne TN
LVHW101926220826
846093LV00009B/383

* 9 7 8 9 3 5 4 6 2 7 4 2 2 *